Cooking in Style
THE COSTCO WAY™

Sautéed Bananas over Ice Cream with Oatmeal-Rum Cookies can be found on page 110.

Cooking in Style
THE COSTCO WAY™

Favorite recipes using Costco products

Tim Talevich
Editorial Director

With a foreword by
Kathy Casey

Issaquah, Washington

Senior Vice President E-commerce and Publishing	Ginnie Roeglin
Publisher:	David W. Fuller
Editorial Director:	Tim Talevich
Art Director:	Doris Winters
Associate Editor:	Judy Gouldthorpe
Graphic Designer:	Dawna Tessier
Photographers:	Darren Emmens Chris McArthur Tom Clements Devin Seferos
Food Stylists:	Amy Muzyka-McGuire Jane Morimoto Chris Jackson Joanne Naganawa
Kitchen Manager:	Linda Carey
Studio Assistant:	Sheereen Hitner
Business Manager:	Jane Klein-Shucklin
Advertising Manager:	Steve Trump
Advertising Assistant:	Linda Collins
Production Manager:	Pam Sather
Assistant Production Manager:	Antolin Matsuda
Color Specialist:	MaryAnne Robbers
Print Management:	Jim Letzel, Will Ting, GSSI
Proofreader:	Shana McNally
Distribution:	Rossie Cruz

All photographs by Iridio Photography,
with the following exceptions:
Diamond Fruit Growers, 44 (top left)
Kathy Casey Studios, 68 (top left)
Swift & Company, 77, 78, 79
Lori Balse, 95 (chef photo)
Photodisc, 100 (bottom right)
Getty Images, 103 (top right)
Pom Wonderful, 181
Starbucks, 213
Swift & Company, back cover

FIRST EDITION

Photography by Iridio Photography, Seattle
Printed by Toppan Printing Co., Ltd. — Japan

ISBN-13: 978-0-9722164-6-3
ISBN-10: 0-9722164-6-4
Library of Congress Control Number: 2006931110

31

89

45

176

Contents

To Our Valued Members ▮

We are very pleased to offer our fifth cookbook, *Cooking in Style The Costco Way*. As in past years, we have published a book of our favorite recipes using food items found in Costco. We're delighted to offer this gift to you as a thank-you for your business and your loyal membership.

This book has been made possible through the support of Costco's many food suppliers. We've asked our suppliers to develop recipes to showcase their products, focusing on a stylishly simple approach that will help you to entertain your family and friends without spending all your time in the kitchen. My personal party-plan tip is to make a few of the great dishes in this book and then fill in the rest with fresh and prepared items from Costco!

At Costco, you'll find only top-quality foods that you'll be proud to serve to your guests. Our buyers constantly work with our food suppliers to improve the quality and value of our products. At Costco, that improvement is known as a "Salmon Story," named after improvements we have made over the years in the quality of our salmon fillets, while at the same time reducing the price. We're working on many new Salmon Stories throughout our warehouses and in our fresh meat, seafood, produce, gourmet deli and bakery departments.

We hope you enjoy this book, and we encourage you to show off your own style preparing some of our favorite products.

Bon appétit!

Ginnie Roeglin,
Senior Vice President,
E-commerce and Publishing

Wow! The Costco cookbooks just keep getting better! This is the fifth, with beautiful food photography, serving tips and more wonderful recipes using products available at your local Costco.

And what a star-studded celebrity chef and writer lineup in the "Chef's Choice" chapter this year, too! Ten foodie glitterati, including Food Network's Ina Garten and Mario Batali, as well as Deborah Madison, G. Garvin and yours truly, contributed delicious recipes from their personal recipe files. They all do wonderful things with Costco's products.

There are also great dishes created by in-house chefs for many of the brands featured. These chefs are intimately familiar with their companies' products, and their expertise shines through in their recipes.

You'll also find some recipes markedy by a special "Organic" symbol. This symbol means that the product has met certain standards in the growing and manufacturing processes—which is important to many people today. You'll find an increasing number of organic products at Costco.

I know that when I shop at Costco I am always looking for new and exciting things to try—foods that will inspire new culinary adventures. You can be sure that several fresh and delicious items will be found on your tasty treasure hunt. Whether it's some sexy imported cheeses, jumbo king crab legs plump with meat, or a box of ripe juicy mangos, there is always something at Costco to motivate your next dinner party.

More than 1.75 million copies of this new book are being given out this year. I hope one finds its way to your kitchen counter, where it becomes a well-used staple with dog-eared pages and lots of smudges and foodie fingerprints. Here's to another delicious year!

P.S. If you have a friend who missed getting a copy of *Cooking in Style The Costco Way*, he or she can go to the Costco Web site to view the cookbook online. You'll find this edition, as well as the four previous ones, at costco.com under "Costco Cookbook."

Kathy Casey's most recent cookbook is Kathy Casey's Northwest Table. *She is chef-owner of Kathy Casey Food Studios and Dish D'Lish. For more fun recipes and entertaining tips, visit* www.kathycasey.com.

Kathy Casey

About This Book I

Cooking in Style The Costco Way is the fifth in our series of cookbooks designed to showcase the exciting array of foods sold at Costco.

Like the last two in the series, this book is being distributed free to our members on a first-come, first-served basis the weekend after Thanksgiving as a token of our appreciation for their membership. It is our hope that the book will become a permanent addition to members' cookbook collections.

In this volume we have expanded our popular "Chef's Choice" section to include recipes developed by 16 of the country's most renowned chefs. All of these chefs have achieved national renown with cookbooks of their own, shows on The Food Network or exceptional restaurants. Thanks to all of them for helping to make this another exciting addition to *The Costco Way* cookbook series.

The rest of the book is arranged in a simple and direct manner with sections for breakfast, appetizers, salads and soups, side dishes, entrées, desserts and beverages, the same approach we have used the past two years. The index at the back of the book contains listings by recipe and food item. We also have included a "Vendor Listing" section with telephone numbers and Web site addresses for all of the participating food suppliers.

Every recipe in *Cooking in Style The Costco Way* has been identified with the vendor's name and logo. We want to thank each of these vendors for their support of this book. (Please note that some branded products may not be sold in your part of the country. In such cases, you should substitute a similar product.)

If you have not been able to obtain a copy of this or our other *The Costco Way* cookbooks, or if you have friends or family who might be interested in them, all of the more than 1,000 recipes in the series can now be viewed online at *www.costco.com*. Simply go to the home page and click on "Costco Cookbook."

I hope you will have many satisfying meals incorporating the recipes from this volume and that you will tell your friends about cooking in style, the Costco way.

David W. Fuller,
Publisher

Note on Brands
Many of the recipes in this book were submitted by companies that hold copyrights to the recipes and/or trademark applications/registrations on the brands listed in the recipes. Each of the companies represented in this book asserts its ownership of the trademarks, applications/registrations and copyrights it holds on its company name, brands or recipes. Trademark, application/registration and copyright symbols have been eliminated from the titles and text of the recipes by the publishers for design and readability purposes only.

Cooking in Style
THE COSTCO WAY™

Breakfast

Breakfast Monte Cristo Sandwich
HILLANDALE FARMS/NORCO RANCH/
NUCAL FOODS/WILCOX FARMS ◄

2 eggs

2 tablespoons water

Cooking spray

8 slices thick egg bread or Texas toast

4 slices Cheddar cheese

4 slices Swiss cheese

8 slices Canadian bacon

8 slices cooked bacon

6 eggs, scrambled

1. Mix 2 eggs and water in a shallow dish.

2. Coat an electric skillet or frying pan with cooking spray. Preheat electric skillet to 350°F or heat frying pan over medium heat.

3. For each sandwich, dip 2 bread slices in egg wash and place in the skillet.

4. Place 1 slice of Cheddar on 1 bread slice and 1 slice of Swiss on the other bread slice.

5. Briefly warm 2 slices of both Canadian bacon and cooked bacon on a grill or in a pan, then place on top of Cheddar cheese.

6. Place ¼ of the scrambled eggs on the bacon. Top with second slice of bread, cheese side down.

7. Repeat for remaining 3 sandwiches.

8. Continue to grill until golden brown, turning occasionally, until cheese melts. Makes 4 servings.

Recipe created by Willy Ray, Costco Foods Buyer.

6-Layer Breakfast Casserole
JIMMY DEAN ▲

6 large eggs

¼ cup heavy cream

1 teaspoon salt

¼ teaspoon ground black pepper

1 pound Jimmy Dean* Roll Sausage, cooked, crumbled and drained

¼ cup jalapeño pepper cut in ¼-inch dice

½ cup shredded Cheddar cheese

2 tablespoons minced garlic

1 teaspoon ground cumin

3 thick slices of bread

1. Preheat oven to 350°F.

2. Place eggs, cream, salt and pepper in a bowl and beat until well blended.

3. In a separate bowl, combine cooked sausage, jalapeño, cheese, garlic and cumin.

4. To assemble, place ⅓ of the egg mixture in the bottom of a buttered 2-quart baking dish. Place 1 slice of bread on top. Spread ⅓ of the sausage mixture over the bread. Repeat layering, ending with sausage on top.

5. Bake for 15 minutes, or until eggs are set. Makes 4 servings.

* Brands may vary by region; substitute a similar product.

Handheld Quiche
KELLOGG'S ▼

6 Kellogg's Eggo Homestyle Waffles, toasted
Cooking spray
1 cup shredded low-fat Swiss cheese
$1/2$ cup crumbled cooked turkey bacon
$1/2$ cup egg substitute
$1/2$ cup low-fat plain yogurt
2 tablespoons sliced green onions
$1/4$ teaspoon salt
$1/4$ teaspoon garlic powder
$1/4$ teaspoon black pepper

1. Preheat oven to 350°F.
2. Place waffles on a foil-lined tray coated with cooking spray.
3. Sprinkle each waffle with cheese and bacon.
4. Combine remaining ingredients in a bowl and spread evenly over the waffles.
5. Bake for 25 minutes, or until set and lightly browned. Serve hot.
Makes 6 servings.

Blue Cheese and Vegetable Quiche
LITTLE FARM FROZEN FOODS ▼

2 1/2 cups all-purpose flour

1 teaspoon salt

1 teaspoon sugar

1 cup butter, chilled and cut into small pieces

1/2 cup water

1/4 cup milk

3 large eggs

2 large egg yolks

3/4 cup heavy cream

Coarse salt and freshly ground pepper

1 cup crumbled blue cheese

1 1/2 cups Kirkland Signature by NutriVerde Normandy Blend frozen vegetable mix

1/2 cup chopped walnuts

3 tablespoons grated Parmesan cheese

1. In the bowl of a food processor, combine flour, salt and sugar. Add butter and process for 8-10 seconds. With machine running, add water. Pulse just until dough holds together without being sticky, no more than 30 seconds. If the dough is crumbly, add more water, 1 tablespoon at a time.

2. On a floured surface, roll out dough to about 1/8-inch thickness. Fit into a 10- or 12-inch nonstick tart pan, trimming the edges. Refrigerate for 30 minutes.

3. Preheat oven to 375°F.

4. In a medium bowl, whisk together milk, eggs, yolks and cream. Season to taste with salt and pepper.

5. In another bowl, combine blue cheese, vegetable mix, walnuts and Parmesan.

6. Pour the cheese and vegetable mixture into the tart and cover with the egg mixture.

7. Bake until just set in the center, 30-35 minutes. Let cool for 5 minutes before serving. Makes 6-8 servings.

Mushroom Salmon Quiche
GIORGIO FOODS ▲

8 large eggs or 1 16-ounce carton Kirkland Signature Egg Starts

2 tablespoons flour—all-purpose white or whole wheat

2 cups regular or 2% cottage cheese

1 cup shredded cheese, any flavor you like

1 4-ounce can diced green chiles, undrained (optional)

2 4-ounce cans Giorgio, Penn Dutch or Brandywine* mushrooms, either stems and pieces or sliced, drained

1 7-ounce can boneless, skinless flaked salmon, drained

Cooking spray

1. Preheat oven to 375°F.

2. Place eggs in a large bowl and beat; whisk in flour.

3. Mix in cottage cheese, shredded cheese, chiles, mushrooms and salmon.

4. Lightly coat a 10-inch pie pan with cooking spray. Pour egg mixture into the pan.

5. Bake for 45-50 minutes, or until set.

6. Let stand for 10 minutes before serving. Makes 6-8 servings.

Tip: This dish is delicious cold if you have leftovers.

Brands may vary by region; substitute a similar product.

Fried Potatoes with Bacon, Peppers and Onion
BASIN GOLD ▲

4-6 bacon slices

1 tablespoon butter

4-6 medium Basin Gold* russet potatoes, either thinly sliced or small diced

1 green bell pepper, seeded and finely chopped

1 red bell pepper, seeded and finely chopped

1 yellow onion, finely chopped

2 garlic cloves, minced

Salt and pepper

1/4 cup grated Parmesan cheese

Chopped fresh parsley, for garnish

1. Cut bacon in 1-inch pieces and sauté in a frying pan until crisp. Remove from the pan and set aside.

2. Add butter to the bacon grease and melt over medium to medium-high heat.

3. Stir in potatoes, peppers, onion and garlic. Cook, stirring occasionally, until potatoes are tender and lightly browned. Season to taste with salt and pepper.

4. When ready to serve, crumble bacon over the dish, then sprinkle with Parmesan and parsley. Makes 4-6 servings.

Tip: For a heartier dish, place a fried egg on top of each serving.

Brands may vary by region; substitute a similar product.

Asparagus, Roasted Red Pepper and Basil Tart
MICHAEL FOODS ▼

1 cup all-purpose flour
1/3 cup cold butter (do not use margarine), cut in small pieces
1-2 tablespoons cold water
1 cup (8 ounces) Kirkland Signature Egg Starts
3/4 cup half-and-half
1 cup finely shredded sharp Cheddar cheese
1/4 pound fresh asparagus, cut in 2-inch pieces
1/4 cup chopped roasted red bell pepper
2 tablespoons coarsely chopped fresh basil
2 ounces fresh goat cheese
2 tablespoons pine nuts

1. Heat oven to 450°F.
2. Place flour and butter in a large bowl. With a pastry blender, cut in butter until mixture resembles coarse crumbs. Add cold water a teaspoonful at a time until the dough is moistened. Shape into a ball.
3. On a lightly floured surface, roll the dough into a 12-inch circle. Press into an ungreased 10-inch tart pan with a removable bottom. Line the crust with aluminum foil and pastry weights or dried beans.
4. Bake for 6-8 minutes, or until the edges are light golden brown.
5. Meanwhile, stir together Egg Starts and half-and-half in a small bowl. Set aside.
6. Reduce oven temperature to 400°F. Remove pie weights and foil from crust.
7. Sprinkle bottom of crust with grated Cheddar. Arrange asparagus, roasted pepper and basil over the cheese.
8. Carefully pour egg mixture over vegetables. Drop teaspoonfuls of goat cheese randomly over the egg mixture. Sprinkle with pine nuts.
9. Bake for 30-35 minutes, or until eggs are set in the center. Makes 8 servings.

Shortcut: Use 1 refrigerated piecrust (from 15-ounce box) in place of homemade crust. Unroll dough, press into tart pan and bake as directed above.

Bagels with Smoked Salmon
KIRKLAND SIGNATURE ▲

4 bagels
2 ounces cream cheese (natural or with chives)
12 slices Kirkland Signature Smoked Salmon
1 jar capers
1 red onion, thinly sliced
Chopped fresh dill

1. Slice bagels in half horizontally and spread with cream cheese.
2. Place 3 slices of smoked salmon on the bottom half of each bagel.
3. Top with capers and red onion rings.
4. Garnish with dill and cover with top halves of the bagels. Makes 4 servings.

Crunchy Organic Apple Toppers
FRESH INNOVATIONS ▲

1 slice whole-grain or multi-grain bread
1-2 tablespoons organic peanut butter (crunchy or smooth)
4-5 Organic Prize Slice* Red (Sweet) Apple Slices ⬡Organic

ADDITIONAL TOPPING OPTIONS
Sliced fresh bananas
Banana chips
Chopped peanuts or other chopped nuts
Raisins

1. Toast bread.
2. While still warm, spread toast with peanut butter.
3. Top with apple slices. If desired, add any other topping options.
Makes 1 serving.
Tips: These crunchy Toppers are a delicious, nutritious alternative for breakfast or a snack. For lunch boxes, simply prepare with untoasted bread and serve close-faced.

* Brands may vary by region; substitute a similar product.

Italian Sausage and Egg Pie
NEW YORK STYLE SAUSAGE ▼

Pastry dough for single-crust 9-inch pie
1 tablespoon light olive oil
1 tablespoon finely chopped shallots
1 tablespoon finely chopped onion (optional)
12 ounces mild or hot Italian New York Style Sausage*, casings removed
8 large eggs
1 10-ounce box frozen chopped spinach, thawed and squeezed dry
Pinch of salt
1/4 teaspoon ground black pepper
1/4 teaspoon granulated garlic
1/4 teaspoon dried basil or 1 tablespoon chopped fresh basil
2 tablespoons finely chopped fresh Italian parsley
2 tablespoons grated Romano cheese (or Asiago or Parmesan)
1/2 cup shredded mild provolone cheese (or Swedish Fontina)

1. Preheat oven to 350°F.
2. Line a 9-inch pie pan with pastry dough.
3. Preheat a nonstick frying pan over medium heat. Add olive oil, shallots and onion to the pan. When it starts to sizzle, add sausage and cook, stirring to crumble into small pieces. Cook just until all the pink is gone. Drain off any liquid and set aside to cool.
4. Place eggs in a large bowl and whisk well. Add spinach, seasonings and cheese, and stir until well blended. Fold in cooled sausage.
5. Pour the filling into the pie shell, leaving at least 1/8-1/4 inch of room at the top.
6. Bake for 35-40 minutes, or until crust is golden brown and filling is set in the center. Let cool on a rack. Makes 6-8 servings.

Brands may vary by region; substitute a similar product.

Cameo Apple-Topped French Toast
RAINIER FRUIT

4 large eggs
1/3 cup milk
2 tablespoons sugar
1 teaspoon vanilla extract
1/4 teaspoon ground cinnamon
8 thick slices of bread
2 tablespoons butter, divided
1/2 cup chopped walnuts or pecans (optional)

CAMEO APPLE TOPPING

3 tablespoons butter
4 Cameo apples, peeled, cored and sliced
2/3 cup packed light brown sugar
1/8 teaspoon ground cinnamon

1. Beat eggs, milk, sugar, vanilla and cinnamon together in a large bowl. Soak bread slices in the mixture for 5 minutes, or until saturated.
2. Meanwhile, prepare Cameo Apple Topping: Melt butter in a skillet over medium heat. Add apples and cook for 5 minutes, stirring frequently. Add brown sugar and cinnamon; cook for 2 minutes, or until apples are slightly soft.
3. Heat 1 tablespoon butter in a large skillet over medium heat.
4. Press each bread slice into chopped nuts to coat. Cook 2-3 slices at a time until golden brown on each side, adding butter to the skillet as needed.
5. Serve hot with Cameo Apple Topping. Makes 4 servings.

Stuffed French Toast with Three-Berry Compote
RADER FARMS

6-8 1-inch-thick bread slices
Butter

STUFFING
1 pint ricotta cheese
1/4 cup sour cream
1 tablespoon brown sugar
1 teaspoon grated orange peel
1/2 teaspoon ground cinnamon
1/4 cup chopped walnuts

BATTER
6 large eggs
1/2 cup milk
1/2 teaspoon grated orange peel

1 tablespoon orange juice
1/2 teaspoon vanilla extract
1/2 teaspoon ground cinnamon
1/8 teaspoon grated nutmeg

COMPOTE
1/2 cup plus 2 tablespoons orange juice
1/4 cup granulated sugar
1/2 teaspoon ground cinnamon
1/2 teaspoon grated orange peel
4 cups frozen Nature's Three Berries
1 tablespoon cornstarch

1. To prepare stuffing, combine all ingredients in a bowl.
2. To prepare batter, mix all ingredients in a bowl.
3. Cut a pocket through one edge of each bread slice with a serrated knife and fill with stuffing. Dip into batter and fry in a lightly buttered skillet over medium heat until golden.
4. To prepare compote, place 1/2 cup orange juice, sugar, cinnamon and orange peel in a saucepan and bring to a light boil. Add frozen berries and return to boil. Mix cornstarch with 2 tablespoons orange juice and stir into compote.
5. Serve warm compote over stuffed toast. Makes 6 servings.

RADER FARMS
Family Owned Since 1941

Golden Apple French Toast
YAKIMA FRESH ▼

1 Yakima Fresh* Fuji or Granny Smith apple, cored and sliced
1/2 cup apple juice
1 tablespoon cold water
1 teaspoon cornstarch
1/8 teaspoon ground cardamom
2 large eggs, beaten
1/4 teaspoon vanilla extract
4 slices bread

1. In a small saucepan, combine apple slices and apple juice; heat to a simmer. Cover and simmer until apples are tender but still retain their shape, about 8 minutes. With a slotted spoon, remove apple slices and reserve.

2. Combine water, cornstarch and cardamom, and whisk into apple juice in the saucepan. Heat mixture to a boil over medium-high heat and cook, stirring, until thickened and syrupy. Remove from the heat and set aside while preparing French toast.

3. Heat a large nonstick skillet over medium heat.

4. In a wide, shallow bowl, combine eggs and vanilla.

5. Dip 2 bread slices in the egg mixture, coating both sides. Cook in the skillet until golden brown on both sides. Remove to a serving plate. Repeat with remaining egg mixture and bread slices.

6. Arrange apple slices on top of French toast and drizzle with reserved syrup. Makes 4 servings.

* Brands may vary by region; substitute a similar product.

Grape and Orange Breakfast Crepes
DELANO FARMS ◀

CREPES

3 teaspoons butter, divided
1/3 cup whole milk
3 tablespoons flour
1 large egg
2 teaspoons sugar
1/8 teaspoon ground cinnamon

TOPPING

1 tablespoon butter
2 tablespoons sugar
1 tablespoon orange juice (frozen)
1/2 cup Delano Farms* seedless grapes, sliced in half
1 seedless orange, peeled and sectioned

1/4 cup vanilla-flavored yogurt
Kirkland Signature Granola Snack Mix

1. To prepare the crepes, melt 2 teaspoons butter; let cool. In a bowl, whisk together milk, flour, egg, sugar, cinnamon and melted butter. Refrigerate batter for about 20-30 minutes.

2. Meanwhile, prepare the topping. Melt butter in a heavy skillet over medium heat. Add sugar and orange juice; cook, stirring, until sugar melts. Add grapes and orange sections; heat just until warmed through. Remove from the heat and cover.

3. To cook the crepes, brush a 10-inch nonstick skillet with a little of the remaining butter. Heat pan over medium-high heat to very warm but not smoking. Lift pan off the heat and pour in 1/4 cup batter, tilting all the while to distribute batter evenly. Return skillet to the heat and cook just until the crepe is set and the edges are golden. Turn heat to medium, carefully flip the crepe and cook until the underside is done, about 15-20 seconds more. Transfer crepe to a plate and repeat process with remaining batter (makes 2-3 crepes).

4. To serve, fold each crepe into quarters. Pour the fruit mixture over the crepes. Top with yogurt and granola clusters. Makes 1 serving.

Recipe created by Linda Carey, culinary specialist.
* Brands may vary by region; substitute a similar product.

Bagel Pudding
EINSTEIN BROTHERS BAGELS/ NOAH'S BAGELS ▲

3 Kirkland Signature plain bagels
3 large eggs
1 1/4 cups 2% or whole milk
1/2 cup half-and-half
1/4 cup sugar
1 1/2 teaspoons ground cinnamon
1 tablespoon vanilla extract
1/2 cup pecan halves (optional)
Butter

1. Cut bagels into 1/2- to 1-inch cubes. Spread out on a cookie sheet and let dry overnight.

2. Place eggs, milk, half-and-half, sugar, cinnamon, vanilla and pecans in a large bowl and blend thoroughly. Add bagel cubes and mix gently by hand.

3. Liberally butter the bottom and sides of an 8-inch round cake pan.

4. Pour the contents of the bowl into the pan and spread evenly. Cover with plastic wrap and refrigerate for at least 3 hours and up to overnight.

5. Preheat oven to 350°F.

6. Remove plastic wrap and bake pudding for 20-25 minutes, or until golden brown and firm to the touch. Makes 6 servings.

Tips: To serve 12, double the amount of all ingredients, place in a 13-by-9-inch pan, and bake for 25-30 minutes. Garnish with berries if desired.

 NOAH'S BAGELS

Breakfast Cream Biscuits with Citrus Compote
DELANO FARMS

3 ¾ cups flour
2 tablespoons baking powder
2 teaspoons salt
3 tablespoons sugar
2 ¼ cups heavy cream
1 large egg
1 tablespoon water

CITRUS COMPOTE

4 navel oranges, peeled and sectioned, pith and membrane removed
2 pink grapefruit, peeled and sectioned, pith and membrane removed
1 ½ cups Delano Farms* red and green seedless grapes, quartered
¼ cup sugar

1. Preheat oven to 400°F.
2. Place flour, baking powder, salt and sugar in a bowl and stir to blend. Add cream and stir just until combined.

3. Gather dough into a ball and place on a lightly floured surface. Pat into a round about ¾-inch thick. Cut into shapes with a biscuit cutter and place on a parchment-lined baking sheet. Beat egg with water; brush biscuits with egg wash.
4. Bake for 18-20 minutes, or until golden brown.
5. Meanwhile, prepare Citrus Compote: Combine oranges, grapefruit, grapes and sugar in a heavy saucepan. Cook over medium-high heat, stirring, until sugar melts and the mixture starts to boil. Lower heat and simmer for 5 minutes. Remove from heat and let cool.
6. Serve compote with warm biscuits and butter. Makes 6-8 servings.

Recipe created by Linda Carey, culinary specialist.
* Brands may vary by region; substitute a similar product.

DELANO FARMS

Breakfast Banana Split
FRESH DEL MONTE PRODUCE ▼

1 medium Del Monte* banana
3-6 ounces light vanilla yogurt
1 cup assorted bite-size pieces of fresh fruit from Del Monte*:
    cantaloupe, honeydew, grapes and Del Monte Gold Extra
    Sweet pineapple
1/2 cup low-fat granola

1. Peel banana, cut in half lengthwise and place in a bowl.
2. Pour yogurt in the middle of the banana.
3. Place assorted fruit on top of the yogurt.
4. Sprinkle with granola. Makes 1 serving.

Brands may vary by region; substitute a similar product.

Peach, Nectarine, Plum and Grape Breakfast Pastry
FOWLER PACKING

3 cups sliced Fowler Packing* peaches, nectarines, plums or red grapes (or a combination)
2 tablespoons plus 1/2 cup sugar, divided
4 tablespoons butter, softened
1 teaspoon ground cinnamon
1 package frozen puff pastry sheets, thawed
1 large egg
1 tablespoon water
Confectioners' sugar (optional)

1. Mix sliced fruit and 2 tablespoons sugar in a bowl.
2. In another bowl, combine butter, 1/2 cup sugar and cinnamon; beat until well blended.
3. Unwrap 1 pastry sheet and spread half of butter mixture down the middle third. Spread half of sliced fruit over butter.
4. On each side of the fruit, beginning at the fold, cut 7-8 diagonal lines down the pastry. Fold each piece toward the center, alternating from side to side, from top to bottom of pastry. Crimp the top and bottom. Repeat process for second pastry.
5. Beat egg with water and brush on top of pastry. Place on a baking sheet lined with parchment paper and bake according to package directions.
6. Remove from oven when golden brown and let cool. Dust with confectioners' sugar if desired. Makes 6 servings.

Recipe created by Linda Carey, culinary specialist.
* Brands may vary by region; substitute a similar product.

Fresh Fruit Breakfast Parfait
MAS MELONS & GRAPES/STEVCO

1 medium Mas Melons & Grapes* cantaloupe
2 bunches Stevco* red seedless grapes
1 pound fresh strawberries
4 tablespoons confectioners' sugar
1 32-ounce container vanilla yogurt
Fresh mint leaves

1. Peel cantaloupe and cut in 1/2-inch pieces.
2. Remove grapes from stems.
3. Trim and quarter strawberries.
4. Combine fruit in a large bowl and stir in confectioners' sugar. Refrigerate for 10 minutes.
5. Place 3 tablespoonfuls of yogurt in each of 8 deep sundae glasses. Add fruit and top generously with remaining yogurt.
6. Top with fresh mint and serve. Makes 8 servings.

* Brands may vary by region; substitute a similar product.

Ultimate Melt-in-Your-Mouth Pancakes
BISQUICK

2 cups Original Bisquick mix
1 cup milk
1 tablespoon sugar
2 tablespoons lemon juice
2 teaspoons baking powder
2 large eggs
Butter or oil for frying

1. Combine Bisquick, milk, sugar, lemon juice, baking powder and eggs in a bowl and stir until blended.
2. Drop batter by scant $^1/_4$ cupfuls onto a hot greased griddle.
3. Cook until the edges are dry. Turn and cook until golden.
Makes 14 pancakes.

Breakfast

Tropical Breakfast Risotto
SUN-MAID GROWERS ▲

1 1/2 cups water
1 cup instant brown rice
1 8-ounce can pineapple tidbits, drained, liquid reserved
1 12-ounce can undiluted evaporated skim milk
1/2 cup Sun-Maid Natural Raisins
1/2 cup sweetened shredded coconut
1/4 cup sliced toasted almonds
1 medium banana, peeled and diced

1. Combine water, rice and pineapple liquid in a 2-quart saucepan. Bring to a boil over high heat, reduce heat to medium and simmer, uncovered, stirring occasionally, until most of the liquid is absorbed, 7-8 minutes.

2. Stir in milk and increase heat to high. When the mixture boils, reduce heat to medium and cook, stirring occasionally, until most of the milk has been absorbed and the mixture is soft and creamy, 10-12 minutes.

3. Stir in pineapple, raisins, coconut, almonds and banana. Makes 6 servings.

Think-Pink Breakfast in a Glass
SWEET'N LOW ▲

1 cup 2% milk
1/2 cup uncooked rolled oats
1 banana, peeled and quartered
1 cup frozen strawberries (8 berries)
1/2 teaspoon or 1-2 packets Sweet'N Low* Zero Calorie Sweetener
1/2 teaspoon vanilla extract

1. Combine all ingredients in a blender container.

2. Cover and blend at highest speed for 1-1 1/2 minutes. Makes about 2 servings.

Brands may vary by region; substitute a similar product.

Cranberry/Macadamia Crunch Bars
NEWMAN'S OWN/KERRY ▼

Nonstick cooking spray

1 pouch Kirkland Signature/Newman's Own Cranberry
Macadamia Nut Cereal

1 cup honey

1 cup sugar

1 tablespoon dark molasses

1 teaspoon kosher salt

1 teaspoon pure vanilla extract

1 cup extra-crunchy peanut butter

1. Spray a 13-by-9-inch baking dish with cooking spray.

2. Poke the seam side of the cereal pouch 10 times with a fork and then crush with a rolling pin using medium pressure. Pour into a large mixing bowl.

3. Heat honey, sugar, molasses and salt in a 3-quart saucepan over medium heat, stirring occasionally, until it comes to a full boil (200°F on a candy thermometer).

4. Remove from the heat and stir in vanilla and peanut butter. Pour over cereal and mix until coated evenly. Press firmly into the baking dish.

5. Cool for 45-60 minutes. Cut into 24 pieces. Cover the dish with plastic or wrap each bar individually for grab-and-go snacks. Makes 24 servings.

NEWMAN'S OWN®   KERRY   KIRKLAND Signature

Appetizers

Confetti Citrus Salsa
SUNKIST ◀

1 large Sunkist navel orange, peeled, segmented and
 torn into small pieces
1 large Sunkist Cara Cara orange, peeled, segmented and
 torn into small pieces
1 large Sunkist pummelo, peeled, segmented and
 torn into small pieces
1/2 small red onion, finely diced
1 medium jalapeño pepper, minced
1/2 cup minced red bell pepper
3 tablespoons chopped fresh cilantro
2 tablespoons chopped fresh parsley
2 tablespoons Sunkist lemon juice
1 tablespoon extra-virgin olive oil
1 teaspoon minced garlic
1 teaspoon honey
1 teaspoon salt

1. Combine all ingredients in a medium stainless steel bowl. Mix well.
2. Cover and let stand for 1 hour to let the flavors blend.
3. Serve with chips. Makes 4-6 servings.

Tip: This salsa is also delicious with chicken or white fish.

Sunkist

Classic Guacamole
HASS AVOCADO ▲

4 large ripe Hass avocados, pitted and peeled
2 tablespoons lemon juice
1 garlic clove, crushed
1 tomato, finely chopped
1/4 cup finely chopped onion
1/2 teaspoon ground cumin
1/2 teaspoon salt
3 drops hot pepper sauce
Tortilla chips

1. Using a fork, coarsely mash avocados in a bowl with lemon juice and garlic.
2. Add tomato, onion, cumin, salt and hot pepper sauce, and stir to blend.
Adjust seasoning to taste.
3. Serve with tortilla chips. Makes 8 servings.

*Presented by California Avocado Commission, Del Rey Avocado, McDaniel Fruit, West Pak Avocado,
Giumarra, Mission Produce, Index Fresh, Calavo Growers and Chilean Avocado Importers Association.
Recipe courtesy of the California Avocado Commission.*

Portabella and Spinach Quesadillas
MONTEREY MUSHROOMS ▲

1 10-ounce package frozen chopped spinach
4 10-inch flour tortillas
2 cups shredded Cheddar cheese
2 tablespoons butter
6 ounces Monterey* Portabella Mushrooms, cut in $1/2$-inch slices
1 tablespoon minced garlic
1 tablespoon vegetable oil
Guacamole
Sour cream

1. Preheat oven to 350°F.
2. Prepare spinach according to package directions. Squeeze out liquid.
3. Place tortillas on a baking sheet, sprinkle with cheese and bake until cheese has melted, approximately 4 minutes.
4. Melt butter in a frying pan over medium heat. Add mushrooms and garlic and cook, stirring, for 7 minutes. Mix in spinach and cook for 3 minutes, or until mushrooms are tender.
5. Divide the mixture among the tortillas and then fold tortillas in half.
6. Heat oil in a frying pan over medium heat and fry the quesadillas until golden brown, about 3 minutes per side.
7. Cut into wedges and serve with guacamole and sour cream.
Makes 4-6 servings.

Brands may vary by region; substitute a similar product.

Mini-Pizza Bruschetta
GRACE BAKING ▲

1 loaf Grace Baking* Pugliese artisan bread
$2/3$ cup olive oil
4 garlic cloves, peeled
2 cups Italian tomato or pasta sauce
4 cups grated mozzarella cheese
1 cup chopped fresh basil

1. Preheat broiler or grill.
2. Cut bread into $1/2$-inch slices.
3. Brush each slice lightly with olive oil. Toast slices under a broiler or on a grill until light golden brown.
4. Rub warm grilled bread with garlic cloves. Drizzle with olive oil, and spoon about 2 tablespoons tomato or pasta sauce onto each slice of toasted bread. Sprinkle with cheese.
5. Return to the broiler or grill for 4-5 minutes, or until golden and bubbly.
6. Garnish with chopped basil and serve immediately. Makes 16 servings.

Brands may vary by region; substitute a similar product.

Hot Artichoke and Spinach Dip
NONNI'S ▲

1 ½ cups canned artichoke hearts, drained and chopped
½ cup mayonnaise
½ cup sour cream
5 ounces frozen chopped spinach, thawed and squeezed dry
¾ cup grated Parmesan cheese
¾ cup grated mozzarella cheese
1 teaspoon minced roasted garlic
1 package Nonni's* Panetini

GARNISH
Chopped fresh tomatoes, chopped fresh parsley and grated
  Parmesan cheese (optional)

1. Preheat oven to 375°F.
2. In a bowl, combine artichoke hearts, mayonnaise, sour cream, spinach, Parmesan, mozzarella and garlic. Mix until thoroughly blended and transfer to a shallow baking dish.
3. Bake for 22 minutes, or until slightly browned.
4. Garnish, if desired, with tomatoes, parsley and Parmesan cheese.
5. Serve hot with a side of Nonni's Panetini for dipping. Makes 8 servings.
Brands may vary by region; substitute a similar product.

Italian Bruschetta with Feta and Capers
DiMARE FRESH ▲

Extra-virgin olive oil
6 ½-inch-thick diagonal slices of Italian or other crusty bread
1 garlic clove, cut in half

TOPPING
1 pound large round tomatoes, cored, seeded and chopped
2 ounces crumbled feta cheese
2 tablespoons balsamic vinegar
2 tablespoons extra-virgin olive oil
2 teaspoons small capers, drained
2 tablespoons chopped Italian parsley
2 tablespoons chopped fresh basil
1 garlic clove, minced
Kosher salt and freshly ground black pepper
Sprinkle of red pepper flakes (optional)

1. Preheat broiler or grill.
2. Brush olive oil on one side of bread slices. Place under the broiler until toasted and brown, being careful not to burn. Remove from the oven, brush the other side with olive oil, and repeat broiling procedure. Remove from the oven and set aside. (This step can be done in advance.)
3. Combine topping ingredients in a small bowl. Mix to blend well.
4. To serve, rub garlic clove on bread slices and top with tomato mixture, draining some of the juices if desired. Serve immediately. Makes 6 servings.
Variation: Place bruschetta under the broiler until cheese starts to melt.

Provolone, Sun-Dried Tomato and Pancetta Galettes
BELGIOIOSO ▲

1 sheet puff pastry, cut into 2 equal rounds
³/₄ cup diced sun-dried tomatoes in oil
2 tablespoons torn fresh basil leaves
6 pieces BelGioioso Sliced Mild Provolone Cheese
3 slices pancetta or bacon, roughly chopped (about 2 ¹/₂ ounces)

1. Preheat oven to 450°F.
2. Place puff pastry rounds on a parchment-lined cookie sheet and cover with plastic wrap. Set aside.
3. In a small bowl, combine sun-dried tomatoes and basil.
4. Uncover the puff pastry rounds and place 3 slices of provolone in the center of each, overlapping if necessary.
5. Place the tomato mixture on top of the cheese.
6. Sprinkle pancetta over the tomatoes.
7. Gather the puff pastry around the filling, making sure not to cover more than a quarter of the filling with dough.
8. Bake for 20-25 minutes, or until the pastry is lightly browned and the filling is bubbling.
9. Place on a serving dish, cut into wedges and serve immediately. Makes 4-6 servings.

BELGIOIOSO®
(bel-joy-oso)

Southwest Chicken and Bacon Roll-Ups
HORMEL ▲

1 cup garden vegetable cream cheese, softened
1 10-ounce can Valley Fresh* Chunk Breast of Chicken or Chunk White Turkey, drained
¹/₃ cup crumbled Hormel/Kirkland Signature Precooked Bacon or Hormel Premium Real Crumbled Bacon
¹/₂ cup Chi-Chi's* or Herdez* salsa
6 8-inch soft taco flour tortillas

1. In a bowl, combine cream cheese, chicken, bacon and salsa. Gently stir until well combined.
2. Spread chicken mixture on each tortilla. Roll up, wrap in plastic wrap and refrigerate until serving time.
3. To serve, cut tortillas into 1-inch pieces. If desired, serve with additional salsa for dipping. Makes 36 servings.

* Brands may vary by region; substitute a similar product.

Italian Sausage with Roasted Tomatoes and Polenta
PREMIO ▼

2 pounds Premio* sweet Italian sausages
2 tablespoons olive oil
18 ripe plum (Roma) tomatoes, split lengthwise
12 garlic cloves, crushed
1 cup chicken broth
4 tablespoons balsamic vinegar
1 teaspoon dried oregano
1 18-ounce tube precooked polenta
1/2 cup grated Romano cheese

1. Preheat oven to 350°F.

2. Split sausages in half lengthwise, place in a lightly oiled roasting pan or casserole, and roast for 15-20 minutes. Remove sausages from the pan and reserve.

3. Raise oven temperature to 400°F.

4. Add tomatoes to the pan and roast until they start to soften, 10-15 minutes. Stir in garlic.

5. Remove pan from the oven and place on a stovetop burner over medium heat. Add broth and vinegar. Simmer, scraping the bottom, until it starts to thicken. Add oregano, sausages and juices from the sausages.

6. Meanwhile, cut polenta into 1/2-inch slices and heat according to package directions. Arrange polenta on an ovenproof platter. Sprinkle with half of the cheese.

7. Check seasoning of sausage mixture and then spoon over polenta. Top with remaining cheese and bake for 5-10 minutes, or until cheese has melted. Makes 12-16 servings.

* Brands may vary by region; substitute a similar product.

Crab Parmesan Cracker Bread
KIRKLAND SIGNATURE ▲

1 10 3/4-ounce can Campbell's condensed cream of mushroom soup
1 pound (about 3 cups) lump crabmeat, flaked
1/2 cup chopped celery
1/4 cup sliced green onions
1/4 teaspoon grated lemon peel
1 tablespoon lemon juice
12-15 pieces Kirkland Signature Parmesan cracker bread, broken
    into appetizer pieces
1/2 cup grated Parmesan cheese
Paprika

1. Preheat broiler.
2. In a medium bowl, stir together soup, crabmeat, celery, onions, lemon peel and lemon juice.
3. Spread about 2 tablespoons of crab mixture on each piece of cracker bread.
4. Arrange on 2 baking sheets. Sprinkle with Parmesan and paprika.
5. Broil 4 inches from the heat for 2-3 minutes, or until lightly browned. Serve immediately. Makes 12-15 servings.

Grilled Chicken Cantaloupe in Pasta Shells
DULCINEA ▲

2 boneless chicken breast halves
Salt and pepper
6 jumbo pasta shells
1 medium mango, pitted, peeled and chopped
1/2 Dulcinea* Extra Sweet Tuscan Style Cantaloupe,
    peeled, seeded and diced
1/4 cup sour cream
1 tablespoon minced fresh chives
2 tablespoons lime juice
1 teaspoon Dijon mustard

1. Season chicken with salt and pepper to taste. Grill chicken. Let cool, then cut into small pieces. Set aside.
2. Cook pasta according to package directions. Rinse in cold water, drain and set aside.
3. Place mango, cantaloupe, chicken, sour cream, chives, lime juice and mustard in a bowl and stir to combine.
4. Stuff the pasta shells with this mixture. Makes 6 servings.

Brands may vary by region; substitute a similar product.

Ahi Nori Kala Pa'a
TJ KRAFT

4 tablespoons mirin (rice wine)

3 tablespoons shoyu (soy sauce)

1 tablespoon lemon juice

1 teaspoon sugar

2 tablespoons water

1 teaspoon cornstarch

Grated daikon radish (optional)

8 ounces TJ Kraft* ahi tuna
 (block cut, sashimi grade)

1/2 cup Nori Komi Furikake
 (Japanese seasoning mix)

2 tablespoons canola oil

1. In a saucepan, combine mirin, shoyu, lemon juice, sugar, water and cornstarch. Heat over medium heat, stirring, until bubbles cover the surface; set aside. Add grated daikon, if desired.

2. Cut ahi lengthwise into 1-by-1-by-6-inch strips. Roll strips in furikake, coating all sides.

3. Heat oil in a frying pan over medium-high heat. Add ahi strips and sear on all sides.

4. Remove and cut into 1/2-inch-thick kala pa'a (coins), using a sharp, thin blade.

5. Arrange on a plate, drizzle with sauce and serve. Makes 4 servings.

Tip: The more well-done, the more difficult this is to cut. Ideal is a raw interior with a 1/8- to 1/4-inch-deep sear.

Brands may vary by region; substitute a similar product.

Tangy Shrimp Appetizer Skewers
LINDSAY OLIVES

1 1/2 pounds cooked medium shrimp with tails intact

2 pints cherry tomatoes

1 7-ounce jar Lindsay* Manzanilla stuffed olives, drained, or
 1 6-ounce can Lindsay* large black ripe pitted olives, drained

1 cup prepared light Caesar salad dressing

8 ounces smoked mozzarella cheese, cut in 1/2-inch cubes

48 small basil leaves (or 24 large basil leaves, halved)

48 4-inch-long cocktail picks

1. In a large bowl, combine shrimp, tomatoes, olives and dressing, tossing well. (At this point, the mixture can be covered and refrigerated for up to 24 hours.)

2. Skewer 1 olive, 1 shrimp, 1 cheese cube, 1 basil leaf and 1 tomato on each cocktail pick. Arrange on a serving platter.

3. Serve immediately or cover and refrigerate for up to 2 hours.

Makes 24 servings.

Brands may vary by region; substitute a similar product.

Breaded Ravioli
KIRKLAND SIGNATURE/SEVIROLI FOODS ▲

1/4 cup all-purpose flour

2 large eggs

4 teaspoons milk

1/2 -1 cup seasoned dry bread crumbs

12 Kirkland Signature* frozen Four-Cheese Ravioli, thawed

3 cups vegetable, corn or canola oil

1 tablespoon grated Parmesan or other cheese

Prepared marinara sauce or salsa

1. Place flour in a shallow bowl.

2. Combine eggs and milk in a small bowl.

3. Place bread crumbs in another bowl.

4. Gently coat each ravioli with flour. Dip in the egg mixture and then coat with bread crumbs.

5. Pour oil into a heavy frying pan and heat until it sizzles. Fry ravioli 4 at a time for about 2 minutes, or until golden brown.

6. Drain on paper towels and sprinkle with grated Parmesan.

7. Cut ravioli in half, insert a toothpick in each half and serve with marinara sauce or salsa. Makes 4-6 servings.

Tip: The flour can be eliminated and the ravioli coated with just the egg mixture and then bread crumbs.

Brands may vary by region; substitute a similar product.

Cheese Bowl Appetizer
LIT'L SMOKIES ▲

1 pound processed cheese, cubed

4 ounces cream cheese, cubed

3/4 cup dark beer

1/2 cup Dijon mustard

1/2 teaspoon Worcestershire sauce

1/4 teaspoon garlic powder

Pinch of cayenne pepper

1/3 cup finely chopped green onion tops

1 pound Hillshire Farm* Lit'l Smokies

1. Place cheeses in a heavy saucepan and melt over low heat until smooth and blended.

2. Gradually add beer, mustard, Worcestershire sauce, garlic powder, cayenne and green onions. Stir until well blended.

3. Serve the dip warm with Lit'l Smokies. Makes 24-28 servings.

Brands may vary by region; substitute a similar product.

Fire-Roasted Artichokes
OCEAN MIST FARMS ▲

4 Ocean Mist jumbo artichokes
4 tablespoons olive oil
4 tablespoons balsamic vinegar
4 teaspoons brown sugar
2 teaspoons minced garlic
Pinch of salt and dried basil

VINAIGRETTE
¹/₄ cup balsamic vinegar
2 ¹/₂ teaspoons brown sugar
1 teaspoon water
2 tablespoons Dijon mustard
Pinch of salt and pepper

1. Rinse artichokes. Trim off top quarter of each artichoke and half of stem. With shears, snip off remaining petal thorns.

2. Stand artichokes in a deep pot. Add about 3 inches of water. Bring to a boil, cover, reduce heat, and simmer until bottoms of stems are completely soft, about 30-40 minutes.

3. Meanwhile, to prepare vinaigrette, combine all ingredients in a small bowl. Cover and refrigerate until chilled.

4. Combine olive oil, vinegar, brown sugar, garlic, salt and basil in a small bowl. Cut cooked artichokes in half through the stem and remove fuzzy centers. Place cut side up and pour mixture over artichokes.

5. Prepare a charcoal grill. Place the artichokes cut side up on the grill. Grill until leaves are charred, about 15-20 minutes.

6. Serve with vinaigrette for dipping. Makes 8 servings.

Asian Chicken Lettuce Wraps with Gourmet Sauces
OKAMI ▲

For variety, try these favorites in addition to the dipping sauce included with Okami* Lettuce Wraps.

WASABI CREAM SAUCE
¹/₂ cup Mexican cream
3 tablespoons mayonnaise
1 teaspoon wasabi powder

2 tablespoons distilled
   white vinegar
2 tablespoons sugar
1 teaspoon chili sauce

Combine all ingredients and blend well. Makes 8 servings.

PEANUT SAUCE
¹/₂ cup mayonnaise
¹/₄ cup smooth peanut butter
2 tablespoons distilled
   white vinegar

2 tablespoons sugar
2 teaspoons soy sauce
1 tablespoon chopped
   fresh cilantro
¹/₄ teaspoon red pepper flakes

Place all ingredients in a blender and process until smooth. Makes 8 servings.

ASIAN CHICKEN LETTUCE WRAPS

1. Remove meal kit components from package.

2. Pierce fully cooked chicken package with 2-3 holes to vent and place on a microwave-safe dish. Heat on high for 45-60 seconds.

3. Rinse and separate lettuce leaves.

4. To serve, place chicken, crispy rice noodles and sauce in lettuce cups; fold lettuce together.

* Brands may vary by region; substitute a similar product.

Fiesta Shrimp Queso Dip
AMERICA'S KITCHEN ▲

1 tablespoon butter or oil
$^1/_2$ pound shrimp, chopped
$^1/_2$ tablespoon chopped garlic
$^1/_4$ cup diced red bell pepper
$^1/_4$ cup diced green bell pepper
1 pound America's Kitchen* Queso Cheese Dip

1. Melt butter in a skillet over medium-high heat. Add shrimp and garlic, and sauté briefly.

2. Add bell peppers and cook until tender.

3. Stir in the dip and warm over low heat until hot.

4. Serve this dip warm with your favorite crackers, bread or tortillas.
Makes 6-8 servings.

* Brands may vary by region; substitute a similar product.

Blueberry Pesto
NATURIPE ▲

2 cups fresh Naturipe* blueberries, plus more for garnish
1 cup cleaned and packed parsley
$^1/_2$ cup freshly grated Parmesan cheese
$^1/_2$ cup toasted walnuts
4 garlic cloves, peeled
$^1/_4$ cup olive oil
1 8-ounce log goat cheese

1. Place 2 cups blueberries, parsley, Parmesan, walnuts, garlic and olive oil in a blender and process until a paste forms.

2. Spoon the blueberry pesto over the goat cheese, covering the top and letting it drip down the sides.

3. Garnish with fresh blueberries.

4. Serve with crackers or sliced baguette. Makes 8 servings.

Tip: Leftovers can be frozen.

* Brands may vary by region; substitute a similar product.

The Original Party Mix
CHEX ▲

6 tablespoons butter or margarine

2 tablespoons Worcestershire sauce

1 1/2 teaspoons seasoned salt

3/4 teaspoon garlic powder

1/2 teaspoon onion powder

3 cups Corn Chex cereal

3 cups Rice Chex cereal

3 cups Wheat Chex cereal

1 cup mixed nuts

1 cup bite-size pretzels

1 cup garlic-flavor bite-size bagel chips or regular-size bagel chips, broken into 1-inch pieces

1. Preheat oven to 250°F.

2. Place butter in an ungreased large roasting pan and melt in the oven.

3. Stir in seasonings. Gradually stir in remaining ingredients until evenly coated.

4. Bake for 1 hour, stirring every 15 minutes.

5. Spread on paper towels to cool. Store in an airtight container. Makes 24 servings.

Microwave directions: In a large microwavable bowl, microwave butter, uncovered, on high for 40 seconds, or until melted. Stir in seasonings. Gradually stir in remaining ingredients until evenly coated. Microwave, uncovered, on high for 5-6 minutes, thoroughly stirring every 2 minutes. Spread on paper towels to cool.

Cranberry-Orange Mix
CHEX ▲

3 cups Corn Chex cereal

3 cups Rice Chex cereal

3 cups Wheat Chex cereal

1 cup sliced almonds

1/4 cup butter or margarine, melted

1/4 cup packed brown sugar

1/4 cup frozen orange juice concentrate, thawed

1/2 cup sweetened dried cranberries

1. Preheat oven to 300°F.

2. In an ungreased large roasting pan, mix cereals and almonds; set aside.

3. Place butter, brown sugar and juice concentrate in a microwavable measuring cup. Microwave, uncovered, on high for 30 seconds; stir. Pour over cereal mixture, stirring until evenly coated.

4. Bake for 30 minutes, stirring after 15 minutes.

5. Stir in cranberries.

6. Spread on waxed paper or foil to cool. Store in an airtight container. Makes 20 servings.

Salads and Soups

Baby Greens with Glazed Walnuts, Pears and Gorgonzola
EMERALD NUTS/DIAMOND FOODS ▲

6 cups baby salad greens, washed and dried
2 ripe Comice or Anjou pears, quartered, cored and thinly sliced
1/2 cup (4 ounces) crumbled Gorgonzola cheese
1 cup Emerald* Original Glazed Walnuts
Freshly ground black pepper

DRESSING
1 tablespoon balsamic vinegar
1/2 teaspoon Dijon mustard
1/2 teaspoon salt
1/4 teaspoon freshly ground black pepper
3-4 tablespoons olive oil

1. To make the dressing, whisk together vinegar, mustard, salt and pepper in a large salad bowl. Drizzle in oil, whisking until combined.
2. Add salad greens and pears to the bowl and gently toss until lightly coated with dressing.
3. Sprinkle with cheese, glazed walnuts and pepper to taste. Serve immediately. Makes 4-6 servings.

* Brands may vary by region; substitute a similar product.

European Salad
FOXY FOODS ▲

3-4 Foxy romaine hearts, torn into bite-size pieces
2 mangoes, peeled and cubed
2 pints fresh strawberries, trimmed and sliced
3/4 cup raisins or sweetened dried cranberries, or a combination of both
1/2 pound honey-glazed almonds
1/4 cup vinegar
1/4 cup sugar
1/2 cup oil
1 teaspoon salt

1. Combine romaine, mangoes, strawberries, raisins and almonds in a large salad bowl.
2. Place vinegar, sugar, oil and salt in a small saucepan and cook over low heat, stirring constantly, for 5 minutes, or until sugar has dissolved. Remove from heat and let cool.
3. Pour cooled dressing over the salad, toss and serve immediately. Makes 8-10 servings.

Spinach and Berries Salad with Crunchy Granola Topping
BEST BRANDS/MULTIFOODS ▼

6 ounces fresh spinach, torn into bite-size pieces
2 tablespoons balsamic vinegar
2 tablespoons rice vinegar
4 teaspoons honey
3/4 teaspoon curry powder
2 teaspoons Dijon mustard
Salt and pepper
1 cup thickly sliced strawberries
1 cup blueberries
1 small red onion, thinly sliced
Kirkland Signature Granola Snack Mix

1. Wash and dry spinach. Place in a large bowl or on individual salad plates.

2. In a bowl, combine vinegars, honey, curry powder, mustard, and salt and pepper to taste. Whisk together and toss with spinach.

3. Add berries and onion; toss gently.

4. Top salad with granola mix to taste just before serving. Makes 6 servings.

Best Brands Corp.

Mixed Green Salad with Pears, Blue Cheese and Hazelnuts
DIAMOND FRUIT GROWERS

¹/₂ cup chopped, skinned hazelnuts

1 4-ounce bag mixed baby salad greens (about 8 cups lightly packed)

¹/₄ cup dried currants

2 firm but ripe Diamond Fruit Growers green or red Anjou pears

¹/₄ pound blue cheese, crumbled

DRESSING

1 tablespoon white vinegar

2 tablespoons apricot spread (without chunks), melted

2 ¹/₂ tablespoons extra-virgin olive oil

¹/₂ teaspoon salt

¹/₂ teaspoon sugar

Freshly ground pepper to taste

1. Preheat oven to 350°F.
2. Spread hazelnuts in a single layer on a rimmed baking sheet. Roast until barely golden, 7-10 minutes. Let cool.
3. Place salad greens, currants and hazelnuts in a large serving bowl.
4. Combine dressing ingredients and whisk or shake to blend. Taste and adjust the seasoning if necessary.
5. When ready to serve, core and cut each pear into 8 wedges.
6. Give the dressing a last-minute shake and pour over the salad. Toss gently and divide among 4 plates.
7. Scatter cheese over the salads and arrange 4 pear slices around each one. Serve immediately. Makes 4 servings.

FRUIT GROWERS, INC.

Nectarine Salad with Poppy Seed Dressing
WESPAK

DRESSING

¹/₂ cup sugar

¹/₃ cup white wine vinegar

1 teaspoon salt

1 teaspoon dry mustard

1 tablespoon grated onion

1 cup canola oil

1 kiwifruit, peeled and chopped

1 tablespoon poppy seeds

10 cups mixed salad greens

1 small red bell pepper, diced

2 WesPak* nectarines, sliced thin

3 ounces crumbled goat cheese

¹/₂ cup pecans, toasted

¹/₂ cup sweetened dried cranberries, plus more for garnish

Salt and pepper

1. To prepare the dressing, mix sugar, vinegar, salt, dry mustard and onion in a food processor.
2. With the motor running, gradually add oil in a steady stream.
3. Add kiwifruit and mix until dressing has thickened. Fold in poppy seeds.
4. In a salad bowl, combine salad greens, bell pepper, nectarines, cheese, pecans and cranberries. Add salt and pepper to taste.
5. Drizzle salad with dressing to taste and toss to lightly coat.
6. Garnish with a few dried cranberries. Makes 6 servings.

* Brands may vary by region; substitute a similar product.

WESPAK.

Roasted Beet and Hass Avocado Salad with Orange Dressing
HASS AVOCADO ▼

4 medium red beets
Juice and finely grated peel of 2 oranges
4 teaspoons white balsamic vinegar
$1/2$ teaspoon salt
$1/4$ teaspoon ground black pepper
2 large ripe Hass avocados, pitted, peeled and cut in quarters
$1/2$ cup seasoned rice vinegar
8 lettuce leaves

1. Preheat oven to 350°F.
2. Wash beets and trim off stems. Place in a small roasting pan and add $1/4$ cup water. Cover pan with foil and roast beets in the oven for 50 minutes, or until a fork goes in easily with a little resistance.

3. Remove beets from the oven and let cool. Peel and cut into $1/4$-inch chunks; set aside.
4. In a small bowl, prepare salad dressing by combining $1/2$ cup orange juice, 1 teaspoon grated orange peel, vinegar, salt and pepper. Whisk to blend.
5. Dip avocado quarters in rice vinegar.
6. To serve, place a lettuce leaf on each plate. Arrange an avocado quarter on each lettuce leaf. Spoon $1/4$ of the chopped beets over each avocado. Drizzle dressing over all. Garnish with orange zest. Makes 8 servings.

Presented by California Avocado Commission, Del Rey Avocado, McDaniel Fruit, West Pak Avocado, Giumarra, Mission Produce, Index Fresh, Calavo Growers and Chilean Avocado Importers Association. Recipe courtesy of the Hass Avocado Board.

Watermelon Salad with Purple Basil and Fresh Mozzarella
BIG CHUY/JOHN LIVACICH PRODUCE/TIMCO WORLDWIDE/ GEORGE PERRY & SONS/UNITED MELON/GROWER SELECT PRODUCE ▲

2 cups watermelon* balls
2 cups fresh mozzarella pieces
1 cup chopped fresh purple basil (or green)
1 bunch green onions, trimmed and chopped
1/3 cup extra-virgin olive oil
Salt and pepper
Baby greens
Prepared crostini
Balsamic vinegar (optional)

1. In a bowl, toss together watermelon, mozzarella, basil, green onions and olive oil. Season to taste with salt and pepper.
2. Serve over a bed of baby greens with crostini on the side.
3. Drizzle with a bit of balsamic vinegar if desired. Makes 6-8 servings.

Brands may vary by region; substitute a similar product.

Watermelon Citrus Fruit Salad
SEALD SWEET ▲

1 well-shaped medium watermelon
1 honeydew melon
1 cantaloupe
3-4 Seald Sweet* clementines, peeled and segmented
2 cups red or white seedless grapes
2 cups fresh strawberries, hulled and halved
2 Seald Sweet* pink grapefruit, peeled and cut in 1/4-inch rounds

1. Slice watermelon in half on the diagonal. With a melon baller, scoop out balls of watermelon and place in a large bowl.
2. Peel and slice honeydew and cantaloupe into chunks, or if desired use a melon baller. Add to the watermelon.
3. Add clementines, grapes and strawberries to the melon. Mix gently.
4. Scoop out remaining flesh inside the watermelon bowl.
5. Cut grapefruit rounds into flower shapes.
6. Place the watermelon bowl on a large serving platter. Add fruit salad to the watermelon bowl, allowing some to tumble out onto the platter. Decorate the salad with grapefruit flowers. Makes 18 servings.

Brands may vary by region; substitute a similar product.

Seald Sweet®
INTERNATIONAL

Summer Citrus Vinaigrette
ODWALLA

¹/₂ cup Odwalla* orange juice
¹/₄ cup balsamic vinegar or raspberry vinegar
2 teaspoons lemon juice
2 teaspoons Dijon mustard
1 teaspoon reduced-sodium soy sauce or tamari
¹/₄ cup extra-virgin olive oil
16 cups mixed salad greens
Salt and pepper to taste
2 tablespoons chopped fresh mint

1. Pour orange juice, vinegar, lemon juice, mustard and soy sauce into a measuring cup. Whisk in olive oil.
2. Place salad greens in a bowl. Just before serving, season to taste with salt and pepper.
3. Add mint to the dressing and stir to combine. Drizzle dressing to taste onto the salad and toss to coat. Makes 8-12 servings.
Tip: Add 2 tablespoons chopped green onions, chives or basil.

Brands may vary by region; substitute a similar product.

Almond Citrus Salad
ALMOND ACCENTS

DRESSING
¹/₃ cup orange juice
2 tablespoons white wine vinegar
2 tablespoons vegetable oil
1 tablespoon honey
2 teaspoons grated fresh ginger
¹/₄ teaspoon salt
¹/₈ teaspoon red pepper flakes

2 grapefruit, peeled and segmented
2 navel oranges, peeled and sliced
¹/₄ cup finely chopped red onion
6 cups lightly packed spinach leaves, torn into bite-size pieces
²/₃ cup Sunkist* Almond Accents Original Oven Roasted
    sliced almonds

1. To prepare the dressing, combine orange juice, vinegar, oil, honey, ginger, salt and red pepper flakes in a blender. Mix thoroughly.
2. In a bowl, combine fruit, onion and dressing. Set aside for 30 minutes.
3. Line 4 individual plates with spinach.
4. Spoon fruit mixture with dressing over the spinach, dividing equally.
5. Just before serving, sprinkle with sliced almonds. Makes 4 servings.

Brands may vary by region; substitute a similar product.

Romaine Hearts with Roasted Italian Sweet Red Onions
TANIMURA & ANTLE/DENICE & FILICE ▲

2 Denice & Filice Italian sweet red onions
1 tablespoon olive oil
Salt and freshly ground pepper
1 cup balsamic vinegar
$^1/_4$ cup orange juice
4 Tanimura & Antle romaine hearts
2 ounces Gorgonzola cheese

1. Preheat oven to 400°F.
2. Peel and slice onions into $^1/_2$-inch rounds. Place on a baking sheet. Brush with olive oil and sprinkle with salt and pepper to taste. Roast for about 20 minutes, or until browned and tender.
3. Place vinegar, orange juice and a pinch of pepper in a nonaluminum saucepan. Bring to a boil. Lower heat and simmer for 10 minutes. Remove from heat and let cool.
4. Wash romaine. Remove large outer leaves and cut in half lengthwise.
5. Arrange romaine spears on 4 plates. Top with roasted onions. Drizzle with balsamic glaze. Crumble cheese over salads. Sprinkle with black pepper to taste. Makes 4 servings.

Tips: Substitute feta or goat cheese for Gorgonzola. Top with bacon bits for a tasty twist.

Apple Chicken Salad
PENNSYLVANIA APPLE/ NEW YORK APPLE ▲

3 pounds chicken breasts
4 ounces celery, diced
4 ounces onion, diced
1 cup light mayonnaise
5 medium Eastern* Jonagold apples
2 hard-boiled eggs, peeled and diced

1. Place chicken breasts in a large saucepan. Add water to cover, bring to a boil, reduce heat and simmer, covered, until cooked. Remove from the water and set aside to cool. Cut meat into bite-size pieces.
2. In a large bowl, combine celery, onion and mayonnaise.
3. Core and dice 1 apple; add to the bowl.
4. Add eggs and chicken. Stir gently to mix.
5. Slice 4 remaining apples in half horizontally and carefully remove the insides, leaving a $^1/_2$-inch-thick shell.
6. Scoop salad mix into each apple shell. Chill before serving.
Makes 8 servings.

Brands may vary by region; substitute a similar product.

Spinach Salad

BOSKOVICH FARMS ▲

2 pounds Boskovich Farms* Fresh 'N' Quick Spinach
4 eggs, hard-boiled, peeled and chopped
1/2 pound bacon, cooked until crisp and crumbled
1 cup croutons
1/2 cup sliced fresh mushrooms
1 red onion, sliced in thin rings

DRESSING
1 onion, chopped
2/3 cup sugar (or Splenda sweetener)
1 teaspoon salt
1 cup vegetable oil
1/3 cup cider vinegar
1/2 teaspoon ground black pepper
1 teaspoon celery seed
1 tablespoon Dijon mustard

1. Chop or tear spinach into bite-size pieces and place in a large
salad bowl.
2. Add eggs, bacon, croutons, mushrooms and red onion.
3. To prepare the dressing, combine onion, sugar, salt, oil, vinegar, pepper,
celery seed and mustard in a blender. Blend until smooth.
4. Pour enough dressing over the salad mixture to lightly coat. Toss and
serve. Makes 8 servings.

Brands may vary by region; substitute a similar product.

BOSKOVICH
FARMS, INCORPORATED

Soledad Mission Caesar Salad
MANN'S ▲

1/4 cup extra-virgin olive oil
3 tablespoons lemon juice, fresh or concentrate
2 tablespoons red wine vinegar
1/2 teaspoon salt
1/4 teaspoon ground pepper
1/3 cup grated Parmesan cheese
3/4 teaspoon dry mustard
1/2 teaspoon garlic powder
1/4 teaspoon soy sauce
2 tablespoons chopped green onion
3 Mann's* romaine hearts, washed, chopped and chilled
2 cups Parmesan-flavored croutons

1. In a small bowl, combine olive oil, lemon juice, vinegar, salt, pepper,
Parmesan, dry mustard, garlic powder, soy sauce and green onion. Whisk
with a fork. Chill if desired.
2. Place romaine and croutons in a large salad bowl. Drizzle with salad
dressing and toss with salad tongs to evenly distribute the dressing.
Makes 6 servings.

Tip: To serve 4 as an entrée, top with grilled tri-tip steak, chicken
or shrimp.

Brands may vary by region; substitute a similar product.

MANN'S
SUNNY SHORES
Fresh-Cut Vegetables

California-Style Pistachio Salad
SETTON PISTACHIO/SETTON FARMS ▼

1 garlic clove, minced

1 teaspoon Dijon mustard

1 tablespoon balsamic vinegar

6 tablespoons orange juice (1 orange, freshly squeezed)

3 cups mixed baby greens (watercress, arugula, frisée, radicchio, curly endive and edible flowers)

1 tart apple, quartered, cored and sliced

1/2 cup crumbled blue cheese

1/2 cup Kirkland Signature California pistachios, shelled

1. Place garlic, mustard, vinegar and orange juice in a small bowl and whisk to combine. Set aside for 5 minutes to let flavors mellow.

2. Wash and dry greens; divide equally among 4 salad plates.

3. Top greens with apples, blue cheese and pistachios.

4. Drizzle with dressing. Makes 4 servings.

Grilled Hearts of Romaine Salad
ANDY BOY ▲

Olive oil cooking spray

2 Andy Boy* romaine hearts

2 tomatoes, halved

Salt and pepper

4 ounces crumbled blue cheese, or $^1/_2$ cup shredded
 Parmesan cheese

$^1/_4$ cup prepared low-fat balsamic vinaigrette dressing (optional)

1. Preheat grill to medium-high.

2. Spray grill rack with cooking spray.

3. Lightly spray romaine hearts and tomatoes with cooking spray; season to taste with salt and pepper.

4. Place tomatoes and romaine hearts on the grill. Grill tomatoes, turning once, until tender. Grill romaine, turning occasionally, for 5-7 minutes, or until the outside leaves are slightly charred and begin to wilt.

5. Transfer grilled romaine hearts to a cutting board and immediately slice coarsely with a serrated knife. Chop tomatoes.

6. Place romaine on a large platter. Top with tomatoes and blue cheese or Parmesan.

7. Drizzle with vinaigrette. Makes 4 servings.

Tip: Arrange your favorite grilled steaks, chicken breasts or fish fillets on top of this delicious smoky salad.

Brands may vary by region; substitute a similar product.

Panzanella with Marinated Fresh Mozzarella (Tuscan Bread Salad)
MOZZARELLA FRESCA ▲

1 large loaf crusty Italian bread, cut in $^3/_4$- to 1-inch cubes

2 cucumbers, quartered lengthwise, peeled, seeded and diced

10 medium tomatoes, diced

$^1/_4$ medium red onion, thinly sliced

1 bunch fresh basil, coarsely chopped

1 22 $^1/_2$-ounce container Mozzarella Fresca*
 marinated fresh mozzarella balls

$^1/_2$ cup reserved marinade

$^1/_2$ cup red wine vinegar

Kosher salt

Freshly ground black pepper

1. Place bread cubes on a baking sheet and let sit out overnight to dry. This can also be done in a 200°F oven, but take care not to dry to the point where it looks/feels like croutons.

2. In a salad bowl, combine bread cubes with cucumbers, tomatoes, onion and basil; set aside.

3. Remove cheese balls from marinade and set aside.

4. Place $^1/_2$ cup marinade in a mixing bowl. Add vinegar and salt and pepper to taste. Add to the salad, tossing gently. Let stand for 30 minutes.

5. Right before you're ready to serve, add mozzarella balls to the salad and gently mix. Makes 6-8 servings.

Brands may vary by region; substitute a similar product.

Mozzarella Fresca
Family of Fresh Italian Cheeses

Antipasto Pasta Salad
TURRI'S ITALIAN FOODS

1 ½ pounds Turri's frozen tri-color cappelletti
1 pound Turri's frozen penne
¼ pound Genoa salami, chopped in small cubes
¼ pound pepperoni, chopped
½ pound shredded Asiago cheese
1 6-ounce can black olives, drained and chopped or sliced
1 red bell pepper, seeded and diced
1 green bell pepper, seeded and sliced
3 tomatoes, chopped
16 ounces prepared Italian salad dressing with olive oil
Salt and pepper
1 tablespoon grated Parmesan cheese

1. Blanch pasta for 1 minute to thaw and let sit in a colander to drain.
2. In a large bowl, combine pasta, salami, pepperoni, Asiago cheese, black olives, bell peppers and tomatoes.
3. Stir in Italian dressing, salt and pepper to taste and Parmesan cheese.
4. Cover and refrigerate overnight. Makes 10-12 servings.

Cocktail Tomato and Cucumber Salad with Fresh Mint
THE OPPENHEIMER GROUP/ RED ZOO MARKETING

15 Baby Seedless* or 3 large greenhouse seedless cucumbers
½ cup balsamic vinegar
1 ½ teaspoons salt
1 rounded tablespoon sugar
22 cocktail-sized Amorosa* or 4 large beefsteak tomatoes
1 cup diced red onion
¾ cup chopped fresh mint
4 tablespoons olive oil
Salt and pepper

1. Slice cucumbers in half lengthwise, then slice the halves diagonally into ¼-inch-wide pieces. Place in a large serving bowl.
2. In a small bowl, combine vinegar, salt and sugar; mix until granules are fully dissolved.
3. Drizzle dressing over cucumbers and toss to coat.
4. Slice tomatoes in half if using cocktail tomatoes or cut into large chunks if using beefsteaks.
5. Add tomatoes, onion, mint and olive oil to the cucumber mixture; toss to blend.
6. Season to taste with salt and pepper. Makes 10 servings.

Brands may vary by region; substitute a similar product.

Potato Salad
TOP BRASS ▲

10-12 Top Brass* red or gold potatoes
Salt
4 hard-boiled eggs
1 cup Best Foods or Hellmann's Sandwich Spread
1 2¼-ounce can chopped black olives
1 cup finely chopped celery
½ cup mayonnaise, or to taste
Pepper

1. Place potatoes in a saucepan, cover with water and bring to a boil.
Add salt, lower heat and boil gently until just tender. Drain and let cool,
then slice into chunks; you can remove the skin or leave it on.
2. Peel and slice eggs into ½-inch pieces.
3. Combine potatoes and eggs in a large bowl with sandwich spread.
4. Stir in olives, celery and mayonnaise to taste.
5. Season to taste with salt and a pinch of pepper.
6. Refrigerate until ready to serve. Makes 10-12 servings.

Brands may vary by region; substitute a similar product.

Norma's Potato Salad
KIRSCHENMAN/KING PAK ▲

5 pounds Kirschenman* or King Pak* new red potatoes,
   boiled and diced
10 hard-boiled eggs, peeled and chopped
1 cup finely chopped green onions
1 cup finely chopped red onions
2 tablespoons celery seed
2 teaspoons salt
4 tablespoons mayonnaise, or to taste
4 tablespoons prepared mustard, or to taste
½ cup sweet pickle juice

1. Combine all ingredients in a large bowl and mix together.
2. Refrigerate until chilled. Makes 14-16 servings.

Norma Rapp, an employee (controller) at Kirschenman Enterprises since 1983, learned how to make this dish from her mother 65 years ago. The recipe has been in the family for four generations.
Brands may vary by region; substitute a similar product.

Asian Chicken Vegetable Rice Soup
KIRKLAND SIGNATURE ◀

3 cups Kirkland Signature Vegetable Stir-Fry

16 ounces chicken breast meat, cut in ³/₄-inch cubes

2 14 ¹/₂-ounce cans chicken broth

2 tablespoons soy sauce (or reduced-sodium soy sauce)

1 teaspoon toasted sesame oil (optional)

1 teaspoon grated fresh ginger

3 garlic cloves, minced

1 cup instant rice

1. Place vegetables in a 3 ¹/₂- or 4-quart crockery cooker. Add chicken.

2. Combine chicken broth, soy sauce, sesame oil (if desired), ginger and garlic. Pour over vegetables and chicken.

3. Cover and cook on low-heat setting for 8-10 hours or on high-heat setting for 4-5 hours.

4. Stir in instant rice. Cover and cook for 5-8 minutes, or until rice is tender. Makes 6 servings.

Variations: Use seafood instead of chicken. Substitute cooked brown rice for the white rice.

Sausage and Bay Scallop Chowder
PREMIO ▲

3 tablespoons butter

1 cup onions cut in ¹/₂-inch dice

1 bay leaf

Salt and pepper

2 cups peeled potatoes cut in ¹/₂-inch cubes

3 cups chicken broth

2 cups clam broth

4 tablespoons cornstarch

2 cups heavy cream, divided

1 pound Premio* sweet Italian sausages, cooked according to package directions and cut in ¹/₂-inch chunks

1 pound bay scallops, trimmed of side muscle

1 cup green onions thinly sliced on the bias

3 tablespoons chopped fresh parsley

1. Melt butter in a 5-quart sauce pot or small soup kettle over medium-low heat. Add onions and bay leaf; cover and cook until soft, 5-7 minutes. Season to taste with salt and pepper.

2. Add potatoes and cook for 3-5 minutes. Add chicken broth and clam broth, and simmer until potatoes are just tender.

3. In a small bowl, make a paste of cornstarch and ¹/₂ cup cream.

4. Add the remaining 1 ¹/₂ cups cream to the soup and return to a simmer.

5. Gently whisk in the cornstarch mixture and stir until the soup returns to a simmer.

6. Add sausage and scallops. Simmer for 3-4 minutes, or until scallops are cooked. Season to taste with salt and pepper.

7. To serve, sprinkle with green onions and parsley. Makes 4-6 servings.

Brands may vary by region; substitute a similar product.

Louisiana Hot Sausage and Black Bean Soup
EVERGOOD FINE FOODS ▲

2 tablespoons vegetable oil

1 cup chopped onions

3 garlic cloves, minced

1 ¹/₂ teaspoons ground cumin

1 pound Evergood* Louisiana Hot Link Sausage,
     cut into ¹/₂-inch pieces

2 15-ounce cans black beans, undrained

2 cups chicken broth

1 cup orange juice

1. Heat a large saucepan over medium heat until hot.

2. Add vegetable oil and onions. Cook until onions soften and turn slightly golden.

3. Stir in garlic and cumin. Cook briefly, but do not let garlic brown.

4. Stir in all remaining ingredients and bring to a boil. Reduce heat and simmer for 15-20 minutes. Makes 6 servings.

Brands may vary by region; substitute a similar product.

Grape Gazpacho
CASTLE ROCK VINEYARDS ▲

1 small cucumber, seeded and chopped

1 Granny Smith apple, peeled and chopped

1 cup chopped tomatillos

1 pound Castle Rock Vineyards green seedless grapes

1 cup chopped walnuts, toasted

1 cup plain yogurt

1 cup white grape juice

1 teaspoon rice wine vinegar

6 mint leaves

Kosher salt

1. Place half of the cucumber, apple and tomatillos in the bowl of a food processor. Add grapes, walnuts, yogurt, grape juice, vinegar and mint. Pulse 9-10 times.

2. Pour into a bowl. Combine with the remaining cucumber, apple and tomatillos. Season to taste with salt.

3. Refrigerate for 2 hours before serving. Makes 4 servings.

Fresh Spinach, Orzo and Chicken Soup
PACIFIC NATURAL FOODS ▼

4 boneless, skinless chicken
   breast halves, cut in
   1-inch cubes
Sea salt and pepper
2 tablespoons olive oil
1 large yellow onion, diced
2 garlic cloves, minced
1 teaspoon ground coriander
Pinch of ground cinnamon

1 32-ounce container
   Pacific Natural Foods* Organic
   Organic Free Range
   Chicken Broth
2/3 cup orzo
1 tablespoon fresh lemon juice
2 cups fresh baby spinach
1/3 cup grated Parmesan cheese
6 lemon wedges

1. Season chicken with salt and pepper.

2. Heat olive oil in a 4-quart saucepan over medium-high heat. Add chicken and sear until lightly browned; remove to a plate.

3. Reduce heat to medium, add onion and garlic, and sauté until onion softens, about 5 minutes. Add spices and stir for 1 minute.

4. Add broth and bring to a boil. Add orzo and cook until tender, 8-10 minutes.

5. Add chicken, bring soup back to a boil and cook for 1 minute.

6. Remove from heat and add lemon juice. Season to taste with salt and pepper.

7. Divide spinach among 6 bowls and ladle hot soup over spinach. Garnish with Parmesan and lemon wedges. Serve immediately. Makes 6 servings.

Brands may vary by region; substitute a similar product.

Side Dishes

California French Bean Sauté
LOS ANGELES SALAD COMPANY ◄

1 pound Los Angeles Salad Company trimmed French green beans
2 tablespoons olive oil
³/₄ cup diced bell pepper (preferably orange)
¹/₃ cup diced poblano chile
¹/₂ cup chopped peanuts
1 teaspoon cumin seeds
1 ear white sweet corn, boiled, kernels cut off the cob
³/₄ cup diced Roma tomato
¹/₂ cup cilantro leaves
Salt and pepper

1. Cook beans in a large pot of boiling salted water until crisp-tender, about 3 minutes. Drain and transfer to a bowl of iced water to cool; drain. (This can be done ahead of time.)

2. Heat olive oil in a large skillet over medium heat. Add bell pepper, chile, peanuts and cumin; sauté for 1 minute.

3. Stir in corn and beans; sauté for 1 minute.

4. Turn off the heat. Add tomatoes, cilantro, and salt and pepper to taste; toss to combine. Makes 6 servings.

Recipe developed by Chef Jean Pierre Bosc, Mimosa Restaurant, Los Angeles.

Braised Carrots with Cilantro and Curry
GRIMMWAY FARMS ▲

2 tablespoons butter
1 ¹/₂ teaspoons minced fresh ginger
1 garlic clove, minced
1 teaspoon curry powder
¹/₄ cup chicken broth
1 tablespoon mango chutney
1 pound Grimmway* baby carrots
Salt and pepper
3 tablespoons chopped fresh cilantro

1. Melt butter in a large skillet over medium heat. Add ginger and garlic; sauté for 30 seconds.

2. Stir in curry powder, chicken broth and chutney.

3. Add carrots and stir to combine. Cover and simmer until carrots are tender and coated in sauce, approximately 7 minutes.

4. Season to taste with salt and pepper.

5. Garnish with cilantro. Makes 3-5 servings.

Tip: These carrots have a wonderful Indian flavor and can be served as an easy and creative side dish with any meal.

* Brands may vary by region; substitute a similar product.

Antipasto Plate with Lasagna
KIRKLAND SIGNATURE ◀

When serving Kirkland Signature Italian Sausage and Beef Lasagna or Kirkland Signature Meat Lasagna, start the meal with a flavorful antipasto plate.

1 3-pound or 6-pound Kirkland Signature Italian Sausage and Beef Lasagna or Kirkland Signature Meat Lasagna
Bruschetta (crusty Italian bread sliced, toasted, rubbed with garlic and drizzled with olive oil)
Olives marinated in olive oil and herbs
Hot Genoa salami, sliced thin
Cappiello marinated or fresh mozzarella cheese
Fresh basil leaves
Roasted bell peppers marinated in olive oil, garlic and herbs

1. Prepare lasagna according to package directions.
2. Meanwhile, arrange all remaining ingredients on a platter. Serve as a first course. Makes 6-12 servings.

Honey-Glazed Carrots
BOLTHOUSE FARMS ▲

1 pound Earthbound Farm* Mini Peeled Carrots
1/2 cup water
1 tablespoon butter
1/2 cup honey
1/4 cup dark brown sugar
1/2 teaspoon grated nutmeg
1 teaspoon ground cinnamon

1. Place carrots and water in a saucepan, bring to a boil, cover and cook for 3-4 minutes.
2. Drain water from the pan, add butter and simmer for 1-2 minutes.
3. Add honey, brown sugar, nutmeg and cinnamon. Mix and continue cooking, stirring frequently, for 3 minutes, or until the carrots are tender. Makes 4 servings.

Brands may vary by region; substitute a similar product.

Side Dishes

Mille-Feuille of Seasonal Vegetables
BC HOT HOUSE ▼

18 ounces white polenta

3 tablespoons thinly sliced
fresh basil

2 tablespoons grated
Parmesan cheese

Extra-virgin olive oil

3 carrots, peeled and trimmed

Salt and pepper to taste

1/4 cup orange juice

2 eggplants

2 garlic cloves, minced

6 BC Hot House* red bell peppers

6 BC Hot House* yellow bell peppers

3 green zucchini

2 sprigs fresh thyme or 1 teaspoon
dried thyme

13 ounces Gruyère cheese, grated

1. To prepare polenta, follow cooking instructions on the package, stirring in basil and Parmesan just before it is done. Coat an 8-inch square pan with olive oil. When polenta is cooked, pour into the pan and set aside until firm. Use round metal molds to form the polenta into 6 individual servings approximately 3 inches wide and 3 inches high.

2. Preheat oven to 350°F.

3. Massage carrots with oil, salt, pepper and orange juice. Place in the oven in a large oiled roasting pan for about 16 minutes.

4. Massage eggplants with garlic, salt and pepper.

5. Mix together peppers and zucchini with thyme leaves, salt and pepper.

6. Add eggplants, peppers and zucchini to the carrots and continue roasting for 30 minutes, or until tender. Remove from the oven and let cool.

7. Peel the peppers, remove seeds and cut into quarters. Cut each zucchini lengthwise and eggplant into 6 slices.

8. To assemble, place layers of vegetables and Gruyère on top of the polenta. Refrigerate until ready to use.

9. To serve, heat in a 350°F oven for about 20-30 minutes, or until cheese has melted. Makes 6 servings.

Recipe courtesy of Chef Lynda Larouche at Watermark Restaurant in Vancouver, B.C.
* Brands may vary by region; substitute a similar product.

Campari Tomato and Goat Cheese Tart
WINDSET FARMS ▼

1 sheet frozen butter puff pastry, thawed
1/4 cup Dijon mustard
10 large fresh basil leaves
20 Windset Farms* Campari tomatoes, cut in half
1/2 cup goat cheese, crumbled
Salt and pepper
3 tablespoons extra-virgin olive oil

1. Preheat oven to 400°F.
2. Remove pastry from container and perforate the surface with a fork. Place on a baking sheet and bake for 8-10 minutes, or until light golden brown.

Remove from the oven and let cool for 5 minutes.

3. Brush mustard over the entire surface of the tart.
4. Lay basil leaves on top and then arrange tomatoes over the basil.
5. Spread goat cheese over the tomatoes.
6. Season to taste with salt and pepper, and then drizzle olive oil over the entire tart.
7. Return the tart to the oven and bake for 8-10 minutes, or until golden brown. Serve immediately. Makes 6 servings.

Brands may vary by region; substitute a similar product.

windset
FARMS

Side Dishes ▌

Grilled or Roasted Asparagus
VICTORIA ISLAND ▼

1 bunch (2 ¹/₄ pounds) fresh Victoria Island Farms*
asparagus, trimmed
2 tablespoons extra-virgin olive oil
Balsamic vinegar (if grilled)
Coarse salt
Freshly ground black pepper

TO GRILL

1. Preheat grill.
2. Fill a skillet with about 1 inch of water and bring to a boil.
3. Place asparagus in the boiling water and simmer for 1-3 minutes, or until nearly tender. Drain immediately and place in ice water to stop the cooking. Pat dry.

4. Brush asparagus with olive oil and grill over high heat for 2-4 minutes on each side. Remove from the grill, drizzle with balsamic vinegar and season to taste with salt and pepper.

TO ROAST

1. Preheat oven to 400°F.
2. Rinse asparagus under cold water and pat dry.
3. Place asparagus on a baking sheet covered with aluminum foil. Drizzle with olive oil, then toss to coat asparagus completely. Spread asparagus in a single layer and sprinkle liberally with salt and pepper.
4. Roast for 10-12 minutes, or until tender but still crisp. Makes 6 servings.

* Brands may vary by region; substitute a similar product.

Grape and Orange Chutney
KIRSCHENMAN/CAL SALES ▼

1 tablespoon canola oil
1 cup finely chopped red onion
¹/₄ cup cooking sherry
¹/₄ cup vegetable broth
¹/₂ cup Kirschenman* seedless green grapes, cut into pieces
¹/₂ cup Kirschenman* seedless red grapes, cut into pieces
¹/₂ cup Cal Sales* seedless orange sections, cut into quarters
1 teaspoon finely grated fresh ginger
2 teaspoons balsamic vinegar
¹/₂ teaspoon mustard seeds
Salt and pepper

1. Heat oil in a heavy skillet over medium heat. Add onion and sauté until softened, about 3-5 minutes. Add sherry and vegetable broth, and simmer until liquid is reduced to about 1-2 tablespoons.

2. Stir in grapes, oranges, ginger, vinegar and mustard seeds; continue to cook for 1-2 minutes.

3. Remove from the heat and let cool. Season to taste with salt and pepper.

4. Serve with pork or halibut. Makes 4 servings.

Recipe created by Linda Carey, culinary specialist.
* Brands may vary by region; substitute a similar product.

Garlic and Herb Roasted Potatoes with Raita
SKAGIT VALLEY'S BEST PRODUCE/ VALLEY PRIDE/WALLACE FARMS

4 - 4 1/2 pounds unpeeled Washington* Red Potatoes

1 teaspoon salt

1/4 teaspoon black pepper

2 tablespoons finely minced fresh garlic

2 tablespoons minced fresh parsley

1 tablespoon minced fresh dill or 1 teaspoon dried

1 1/2 teaspoons minced fresh thyme or 1/2 teaspoon dried

2 tablespoons olive oil

2 teaspoons Dijon mustard

RAITA

1/2 cucumber, peeled, seeded, and coarsely grated

1/2 cup plain yogurt

3/4 teaspoon minced fresh garlic

1 teaspoon fresh lemon juice

GARNISH

Crumbled feta cheese

Chopped parsley

1. Preheat oven to 475°F.

2. Wash potatoes, then cut into long wedges. Mix salt, pepper, garlic and herbs.

3. In a large bowl, whisk oil and mustard. Add potatoes and toss to coat. Sprinkle in herb mixture, then toss again, coating potatoes evenly.

4. Place potatoes skin side down on a greased baking sheet. Bake for 25 minutes, or until tender.

5. Meanwhile, prepare raita: Squeeze cucumber to remove as much liquid as possible. Mix cucumber with remaining ingredients.

6. Arrange potatoes on a serving platter, dollop with raita, then sprinkle with feta and parsley. Makes 8 servings.

Recipe developed by Kathy Casey Food Studios for the Washington Potato Commission.
* Brands may vary by region; substitute a similar product.

Roman-Roasted Potatoes with Peppers and Onions
ANTHONY FARMS/ALSUM PRODUCE/ RUSSET POTATO EXCHANGE

Vegetable oil cooking spray

3 jumbo unpeeled Wisconsin* Russet Potatoes, cut in 1/4-inch slices

2 small red bell peppers, seeded and cut in 1/2-inch strips

2 small green bell peppers, seeded and cut in 1/2-inch strips

2 medium onions, peeled and cut in 1/2-inch wedges

3 tablespoons olive oil

2 tablespoons balsamic vinegar

4 large garlic cloves, minced

Salt

1. Preheat oven to 450°F.

2. Line a large rimmed baking sheet with aluminum foil and coat with cooking spray.

3. In a large bowl, toss potatoes, peppers and onions with olive oil to coat. Arrange in a single layer on the baking sheet. Roast for 15 minutes.

4. Remove vegetables from the oven and sprinkle with vinegar and garlic. Toss thoroughly and arrange again in a single layer.

5. Continue to roast for 15 minutes, or until vegetables are tender and lightly browned. Season to taste with salt. Makes 8 servings.

* Brands may vary by region; substitute a similar product.

Mushroom and Sausage Bread Pudding
KIRKLAND SIGNATURE/AIDELLS SAUSAGE ▼

4 tablespoons unsalted
   butter, divided

2 large eggs

¾ cup heavy cream

1 ½ teaspoons salt, divided

¾ teaspoon pepper, divided

1 pound Kirkland Signature/
   Panné Provincio French
   baguette, cut in ½-inch cubes

½ cup minced yellow onion

1 garlic clove, minced

1 pound fresh mushrooms, halved
   and sliced thin

4 Aidells* Chicken Apple Smoked
   Sausage Links, chopped

2 tablespoons fresh thyme leaves
   or 2 teaspoons dried

1. Preheat oven to 325°F. Grease a 9-by-11-inch baking dish with 2 tablespoons butter.

2. In a large bowl, whisk eggs into cream. Add ½ teaspoon salt and ¼ teaspoon pepper. Add bread cubes and stir to mix well.

3. In a large skillet, melt 2 tablespoons butter over medium heat. Add onions and sauté for 5 minutes. Add garlic, mushrooms and sausage; sauté until mushrooms are tender. Stir in thyme, 1 teaspoon salt and ½ teaspoon pepper.

4. Add contents of skillet to bread mixture and toss until mushrooms are evenly distributed.

5. Spread mixture in the baking dish and set in a roasting pan. Add enough hot water to the roasting pan to reach halfway up the sides of the baking dish.

6. Bake for 35 minutes, or until set. Remove baking dish from the roasting pan and let cool slightly. Serve directly from the dish. Makes 6-8 servings.

Variation: Place salad greens tossed in olive oil and balsamic vinegar on a plate and top with warm bread pudding.

* Brands may vary by region; substitute a similar product.

94

76

108

85

Chef's Choice

The world's best chefs have the special ability to infuse dishes with their unique personalities. We asked several top chefs to do their magic with the products supplied by these great companies:

Kathy Casey

When not in the kitchen cooking or at the bar creating cocktails, celebrity chef Kathy Casey is busy running her food, beverage and concept-development consulting company, Kathy Casey Food Studios®, based in Seattle. She is also the owner of Dish D'Lish™, a café and gourmet food products company. Her latest book is Kathy Casey's Northwest Table (Chronicle Books, 2006, available at costco.com). For more, see www.kathycasey.com.

Mustard-Rubbed
Lamb Rack with Apple
Mint "Marmalade"

Mustard-Rubbed Lamb Rack with Apple Mint "Marmalade"
AUSTRALIAN LAMB ◄
All recipes developed by Kathy Casey

2 frenched Australian racks of lamb (about 2 ½ pounds total)
Mint sprigs, for garnish

RUB
3 tablespoons whole-grain mustard
2 tablespoons prepared horseradish
2 teaspoons kosher salt
1 teaspoon coarsely ground black pepper
4 garlic cloves, minced or pressed through a garlic press
1 tablespoon minced fresh thyme
1 tablespoon olive oil

MARMALADE
1 tablespoon butter
1 large unpeeled green apple, cored and coarsely grated
1 tablespoon cider vinegar
½ cup red pepper jelly
1 tablespoon minced fresh mint

1. There should be only a thin layer of fat over the meaty side of the lamb racks; if too thick, trim fat carefully with a sharp knife.
2. To prepare the rub, place all ingredients in a small bowl and mix to a paste. Dry lamb well with paper towels, then smear rub on meaty parts. Let sit at room temperature for 20 minutes.
3. To prepare the marmalade, melt butter in a sauté pan over medium-high heat. Add apple and sauté for 4 minutes, or until just tender. Add vinegar, jelly and mint, bring to a boil, and boil for 2 minutes, or until it has the consistency of chutney. Let cool.
4. Meanwhile, preheat oven to 450°F. In a shallow roasting pan, set lamb racks flat, meaty side up. Roast for 20 minutes, or until internal temperature is 135-140°F (medium-rare), or to the doneness you like.
5. Remove from oven, loosely tent with foil and let stand for 5 minutes. Carve into chops, cutting between the bones.
6. Serve 3-4 chops per person. Dollop with marmalade and garnish with mint. Makes 4 servings.
Recipe from Kathy Casey's Northwest Table *(Chronicle Books, 2006).*

Roast Leg of Lamb with Fennel and Orange Rub
AUSTRALIAN LAMB ▲

Finely minced zest of 2 oranges
2 tablespoons toasted fennel seed, ground
1 tablespoon kosher salt
1 ½ teaspoons cracked black pepper
1 tablespoon Dijon mustard
2 tablespoons minced fresh rosemary
2 teaspoons minced fresh garlic
¼ cup extra-virgin olive oil
5 pounds boneless, trimmed Australian leg of lamb

1. To prepare the rub, place grated orange zest, fennel seed, salt, pepper, mustard, rosemary, garlic and olive oil in a small bowl and mix together well.
2. Remove netting from lamb. Rub ⅓ of the rub mixture over the inside surfaces of the leg. Tie the roast together with 3 pieces of string.
3. Place a roasting rack in a shallow roasting pan or sided baking sheet. Rub remainder of rub all over the outside of the roast. Marinate, covered and refrigerated, for at least 1 hour, or up to overnight.
4. When ready to roast, preheat oven to 450°F.
5. Roast lamb for 15 minutes, then turn oven temperature down to 325°F. Continue roasting for about 1 hour, or until internal temperature is 135-140°F (medium-rare).
6. Let the lamb rest for 5-10 minutes before serving. To serve, remove string and cut against the grain in thin slices. Makes 8-10 servings.
Recipe © 2006 Kathy Casey Food Studios

Seared Lamb Chops with Olive Jus
AUSTRALIAN LAMB ▼

OLIVE COMPOUND

4 tablespoons (¹/₂ stick) butter, softened

2 teaspoons Dijon mustard

1 tablespoon minced fresh basil

2 teaspoons minced garlic

2 teaspoons minced lemon zest

2 tablespoons finely chopped Italian parsley

¹/₄ cup pitted kalamata olives, chopped

8 thick Australian loin lamb chops

Kosher salt

Coarsely ground black pepper

3 tablespoons olive oil, or as needed

1 cup chicken stock or demi-glace

Italian parsley sprigs, for garnish

1. To prepare Olive Compound, in a mixer or food processor, whip butter with all ingredients except olives until fluffy and well combined. Mix in olives. This can be made in advance and refrigerated for 1 week, or frozen for 1 month.

2. When ready to cook the lamb, have olive compound at room temperature. Preheat oven to 475°F.

3. Salt and pepper chops liberally on both sides. Heat 1 tablespoon oil in a heavy skillet over medium-high to high heat. When very hot, add 2-3 chops, being careful not to overcrowd. Quickly sear on each side until browned but not cooked through. Transfer to a rack over a rimmed baking sheet. Repeat with remaining chops, using additional oil as needed. Reserve skillet to make sauce.

4. Roast lamb for 20 minutes, or until internal temperature is 135-140°F (medium-rare).

5. Place skillet in which lamb was browned over high heat, add chicken stock/demi-glace and boil liquid for 2-3 minutes, or until reduced to a glaze. Remove from the heat and vigorously whisk in the olive compound.

6. To serve, spoon the sauce over the lamb and garnish with parsley.

Makes 4 servings.

Recipe © 2006 Kathy Casey Food Studios

Ina Garten

In 1978, Ina Garten left her job as a budget analyst at the White House to pursue her dream: operating a specialty food store in the Hamptons. Since opening The Barefoot Contessa, Garten has gone on to star in a Food Network show of the same name and written the phenomenally successful Barefoot Contessa *cookbook series (some available at costco.com). She lives in East Hampton, New York, with her husband, Jeffrey.*

Chicken with Morels
GOLD KIST FARMS ◀
Recipe by Ina Garten from *Barefoot in Paris*

1 ounce dried morels, soaked for 30 minutes in 3 cups very hot water
6 Gold Kist Farms* boneless, skinless split chicken breasts
Kosher salt
Freshly ground black pepper
All-purpose flour, for dredging
¹/₄ cup clarified butter (see note)
¹/₃ cup chopped shallots
1 tablespoon minced garlic
1 cup Madeira wine
1 cup crème fraîche
1 cup heavy cream
2 tablespoons freshly squeezed lemon juice

1. Preheat oven to 375°F. Lift morels carefully from water, leaving any grit behind. Rinse a few times to be sure all grittiness is gone. Dry lightly with paper towels and set aside. Discard the liquid.

2. Sprinkle chicken breasts with salt and pepper to taste. Dredge in flour and shake off excess. Heat half of clarified butter in a large sauté pan over medium-low heat and cook chicken in 2 batches until browned on both sides, 8-10 minutes. Remove to an ovenproof casserole.

3. Add remaining clarified butter to the pan along with shallots, morels and garlic. Sauté over medium heat for 2 minutes, stirring constantly.

4. Pour in Madeira and cook over high heat to reduce liquid by half, 2-4 minutes. Add crème fraîche, cream, lemon juice, 1 teaspoon salt and ³/₄ teaspoon pepper. Boil until mixture starts to thicken, 5-10 minutes.

5. Pour the sauce over chicken and bake for 12 minutes, or until chicken is heated through. Makes 6 servings.

Note: To clarify butter, melt in a saucepan over low heat. Remove white foam on the surface, then let butter sit at room temperature until solids sink. Pour off golden liquid and discard white sediment.

* Brands may vary by region; substitute a similar product.
Recipes reprinted courtesy of Clarkson Potter/Publishers, a division of Random House, Inc.

Grilled Lemon Chicken
GOLD KIST FARMS ▲
Recipe by Ina Garten
from *The Barefoot Contessa Cookbook*

³/₄ cup freshly squeezed lemon juice (4 lemons)
³/₄ cup good olive oil
2 teaspoons kosher salt
1 teaspoon freshly ground black pepper
1 tablespoon minced fresh thyme leaves or ¹/₂ teaspoon dried
2 pounds Gold Kist Farms* boneless, skinless split chicken breasts (about 6)

SATAY DIP
1 tablespoon olive oil
1 tablespoon dark sesame oil

²/₃ cup small-diced red onion
1 ¹/₂ teaspoons minced garlic
1 ¹/₂ teaspoons minced fresh ginger root
¹/₄ teaspoon crushed red pepper flakes
2 tablespoons good red wine vinegar
¹/₄ cup light brown sugar, packed
2 tablespoons soy sauce
¹/₂ cup smooth peanut butter
¹/₄ cup ketchup
2 tablespoons dry sherry
1 ¹/₂ teaspoons freshly squeezed lime juice

1. Whisk together lemon juice, olive oil, salt, pepper and thyme; pour over chicken breasts. Cover and marinate in the refrigerator for 6 hours or overnight.

2. Heat a charcoal grill and cook chicken for 10 minutes on each side, or until just cooked through. Cool slightly and cut diagonally in ¹/₂-inch-thick slices. Skewer with wooden sticks.

3. To prepare the Satay Dip, place olive oil, sesame oil, red onion, garlic, ginger and red pepper flakes in a pot and cook over medium heat until onion is transparent, 10-15 minutes. Whisk in remaining ingredients; cook for 1 more minute. Let cool. Serve dip with chicken skewers. Makes 6 servings.

Variations: Omit the marinade and substitute 2 pounds of Gold Kist Farms marinated boneless, skinless split chicken breasts (Teriyaki, Lemon Herb or Roasted Garlic & Herb). Baste chicken with olive oil during grilling.

* Brands may vary by region; substitute a similar product.

Chef's Choice I

Mexican Chicken Soup
GOLD KIST FARMS ▼
Recipe by Ina Garten
from Barefoot Contessa at Home

4 Gold Kist Farms* boneless, skinless split chicken breasts

Good olive oil

Kosher salt

Freshly ground black pepper

2 cups chopped onions

1 cup chopped celery

2 cups chopped carrots

4 large garlic cloves, chopped

2 1/2 quarts homemade chicken stock

1 28-ounce can whole tomatoes in puree, crushed

2-4 jalapeño peppers, seeded and minced

1 teaspoon ground cumin

1 teaspoon ground coriander

1/4-1/2 cup chopped fresh cilantro (optional)

6 6-inch fresh white corn tortillas

FOR TOPPING

Sliced avocado, sour cream, grated Cheddar cheese and broken tortilla chips

1. Preheat oven to 350°F.

2. Place chicken breasts on a sheet pan. Rub with olive oil and sprinkle with salt and pepper to taste. Roast for 30 minutes, or until done. When the chicken is cool enough to handle, shred the meat. Cover and set aside.

3. Meanwhile, heat 3 tablespoons olive oil in a large pot. Add onions, celery and carrots, and cook over medium-low heat for 10 minutes, or until onions start to brown. Add garlic and cook for 30 seconds.

4. Stir in chicken stock, tomatoes with their puree, jalapeños, cumin, coriander, 1 tablespoon salt (depending on saltiness of chicken stock), 1 teaspoon pepper and cilantro, if using.

5. Cut tortillas in half and then crosswise into 1/2-inch strips and add to the soup. Bring soup to a boil, then lower heat and simmer for 25 minutes.

6. Add shredded chicken and season to taste.

7. Serve hot topped with avocado, sour cream, cheese and tortilla chips.

Makes 6-8 servings.

* Brands may vary by region; substitute a similar product.

Monty Staggs

Monty Staggs is Research and Development Chef for Swift & Company. He learned his craft on the job while serving as executive chef of top-rated fine dining restaurants in Houston and Los Angeles, and later worked as a corporate executive chef for several companies. Staggs has appeared on ABC's Good Morning America as a guest chef, and he was named the Cream of the Crop Chef by the Houston Chronicle.

Cranberry-Sage
Double-Cut Pork Chops

Swift & Company®

Chef's Choice I

Cranberry-Sage Double-Cut Pork Chops
SWIFT ◄

All recipes developed by Monty Staggs

4 double-cut pork chops

BRINE

2 cups hot water

3 tablespoons kosher salt

3 tablespoons dark brown sugar

2 tablespoons minced garlic

1 cup cold water

2 tablespoons black peppercorns

1 teaspoon ground cinnamon

3 whole cloves

1 bay leaf

1 teaspoon ground allspice

2 teaspoons ground coriander

DRY RUB

2 tablespoons kosher salt

1 tablespoon ground black pepper

1 tablespoon dry mustard

1 tablespoon granulated garlic

1 teaspoon light brown sugar

CRANBERRY-SAGE SAUCE

1 tablespoon unsalted butter

1 teaspoon minced garlic

2 teaspoons minced shallot

1 1/4 cups dry white wine

2 tablespoons jus from roasting pan

1 cup whole berry cranberry sauce

1 tablespoon slivered fresh sage leaves

1 teaspoon kosher salt

1 teaspoon ground black pepper

1. To prepare brine, combine hot water, salt and sugar in a bowl. Whisk until sugar and salt dissolve. Add remaining ingredients and refrigerate until chilled.

2. Place pork chops in a large dish, add brine, cover and refrigerate for up to 4 hours.

3. Combine all dry rub ingredients. Remove chops from brine and rub with the dry rub.

4. Preheat oven to 350°F.

5. Place chops on an oiled sheet pan and bake for 14-18 minutes, or until internal temperature is 150°F. Let chops rest for a few minutes before serving.

6. To prepare sauce, heat a saucepan to medium-high. Add butter, garlic and shallot; sauté briefly (do not burn).

7. Add wine and cook for about 2 minutes. Add pan jus, cranberry sauce, sage, salt and pepper. Reduce heat to medium-low and simmer for 30 seconds, then adjust seasoning to taste.

8. Serve sauce with pork chops. Makes 4 servings.

Latin Marinated Cedar Plank Pork Filets
SWIFT ▲

2 pork filets (cut from loin)

1 cedar plank

MARINADE

1/4 cup olive oil

1 cup orange juice

1 bunch fresh cilantro, chopped fine

1/4 cup light brown sugar

1 tablespoon cayenne pepper

1/4 cup paprika

1/4 cup ground cumin

2 tablespoons ground coriander seed

1 tablespoon kosher salt

1 tablespoon finely ground black pepper

1. Place all marinade ingredients and pork in a large zipper-lock bag and shake to mix thoroughly. Marinate in the refrigerator for 4-24 hours.

2. Place cedar plank in water to cover and soak for 2 hours.

3. Preheat grill to medium-high.

4. Place soaked cedar plank over the hottest part of the grill for 3 minutes.

5. Flip the plank to the other side and place marinated pork on the plank.

6. Move the plank over indirect heat and cook for 20-25 minutes, checking every 5 minutes to make sure the plank has not caught fire but is smoldering.

7. Remove the plank from the grill when the pork has an internal temperature of 150°F. Let pork rest for a couple of minutes before serving.

8. Slice pork and serve on the cedar plank. Makes 3-4 servings.

Prime Beef Filet with Black Cherry and Toasted Walnut Sauce
SWIFT ▼

SEASONING RUB

2 teaspoons dry English mustard

1 teaspoon kosher salt

1 teaspoon coarsely ground
   black pepper

1/2 teaspoon granulated garlic

1/2 teaspoon cayenne pepper

2 prime beef filets

1 tablespoon canola oil

2 tablespoons unsalted butter

2 tablespoons dried black cherries

1/4 cup medium walnut pieces

1 tablespoon chopped fresh garlic

1/2 cup dry red wine

1/2 cup beef stock

1 tablespoon prepared cranberry
   sauce

Kosher salt

Freshly ground black pepper

1 tablespoon cornstarch (optional)

1. Preheat oven to 400°F.

2. To prepare the seasoning rub, combine all ingredients in a bowl. Rub each
filet generously with the rub.

3. Preheat an ovenproof sauté pan on the stove over medium-high heat.
Add canola oil to the pan.

4. Place both filets in the pan and sear for about 3 minutes. Turn over and
sear for 2 minutes.

5. Place the pan in the oven for about 5 minutes for medium-rare. Add 1 1/2
minutes of cooking time for each level of doneness. Remove filets from the
pan and let rest.

6. Place the pan on the stove and heat to medium-high. Add butter,
cherries, walnuts and garlic; sauté for about 2 minutes.

7. Add wine and cook until reduced by half. Add beef stock and reduce
by half.

8. Add cranberry sauce and salt and pepper to taste; reduce heat to medium-low
so the sauce simmers.

9. For a thicker sauce, mix cornstarch with 2 tablespoons water to create a
slurry. Add a teaspoon of the slurry to the sauce and stir for 10 seconds.
Repeat until desired consistency is achieved. Makes 2 servings.

G. Garvin

G. Garvin's series, Turn Up the Heat with G. Garvin, *premiered on TV One, the lifestyle and entertainment cable network for African-American adults, in 2004, and he has quickly made a name for himself on TV just as he has in the world of fine dining. Southwest Airlines' magazine,* Spirit, *ranked Garvin as the third-best TV chef. His first cookbook is* Turn Up the Heat with G. Garvin *(Meredith Books, 2006, available at costco.com).*

Rigatoni Filetto
TARANTINO ◄
Recipe developed by G. Garvin

10 whole plum tomatoes
8 garlic cloves
1/4 cup olive oil
8 ounces pancetta or bacon, cut into thin strips
2 Tarantino's* mild Italian sausages, casings removed
1 large onion, diced
2 tablespoons chopped shallots
1/2 cup white wine
2 tablespoons chopped fresh basil
Salt
Black pepper
1 16-ounce box rigatoni
1 tablespoon unsalted butter
Shredded Parmesan cheese

1. Preheat oven to 375°F. In a large pot, bring 2 quarts of water with a dash of salt to a boil.
2. Core tomatoes and place in a roasting pan with garlic cloves. Add olive oil and stir to coat. Roast tomatoes and garlic until garlic is golden brown, rotating them in the pan to cook evenly. Remove from the oven; let cool. Remove tomatoes and garlic from the pan and chop; set aside.
3. Pour the oil from the roasting pan into a large saucepan and heat over medium heat. Add pancetta and sausage to the pan and cook, stirring to break up sausage, until browned.
4. Add onion and shallots; cook until tender. Stir in tomatoes and garlic, wine and basil. Simmer for 10-15 minutes. Season to taste with salt and pepper.
5. While the sauce simmers, add rigatoni to boiling water and cook according to package directions.
6. To finish the sauce, stir in butter until melted. Drain pasta and add to the sauce; mix well.
7. Top each serving with shredded Parmesan. Makes 6 servings.
* Brands may vary by region; substitute a similar product.

Pigs in a Square
TARANTINO ▲

12 Tarantino's* breakfast sausage links
4 sheets prepared puff pastry
12 slices Cheddar cheese

MUSTARD DIPPING SAUCE
1/4 cup Dijon mustard

4 tablespoons honey mustard
1/2 cup mayonnaise
1 tablespoon Worcestershire sauce
2 tablespoons prepared horseradish sauce
1 teaspoon hot pepper sauce

1. Cook sausages in a skillet over medium heat; remove from the pan and let cool.
2. Preheat oven to 400°F.
3. Cut pastry sheets into 24 rectangles slightly larger than sausages. Place a slice of cheese in the center of each pastry rectangle and top with a sausage. Top with another piece of pastry. Fold down one corner and pinch the edges together.
4. Place on a baking sheet and bake for 15-18 minutes, or until pastry is golden and puffed.
5. To prepare the dipping sauce, mix all ingredients in a bowl.
6. Serve the pigs with the dipping sauce. Makes 6 servings.
Variation: Place each sausage link on the corner of a cheese-covered pastry square and roll up. This version requires half the amount of puff pastry.
Recipe created by Linda Carey, culinary specialist.
* Brands may vary by region; substitute a similar product.

Chef's Choice I

Meat Lover's Stew
TARANTINO ▼
Recipe developed by G. Garvin

1/4 cup olive oil

8 ounces boneless, skinless chicken breast, chopped

3 tablespoons chopped garlic

2 tablespoons chopped shallots

1 teaspoon salt, divided

1 teaspoon ground black pepper, divided

8 ounces beef steak, cubed

8 ounces boneless lamb, cubed

2 large potatoes, cubed

3 tablespoons curry powder

3 carrots, chopped

2 zucchini, sliced

1 yellow bell pepper, diced

1 onion, chopped

3 Tarantino's* mild Italian sausages, sliced

5 garlic cloves

6 cups water

1 cup white wine

1 cup beef stock

1 cup halved grape tomatoes

8 ounces green peas (fresh or frozen)

1. In a large pot, heat olive oil over medium heat. Add chicken, garlic, shallots, 1/2 teaspoon salt and 1/2 teaspoon pepper. Cook, stirring, until chicken starts to brown.

2. Add steak, lamb, potatoes and curry powder; mix well. Stir in carrots, zucchini, bell pepper and onion. Add sausage, garlic cloves and remaining 1/2 teaspoon salt and pepper. Stir in water, wine and beef stock.

3. Bring to a simmer. Add grape tomatoes and peas. Cover, reduce heat and let simmer for 20-30 minutes, or until vegetables are tender. Stir and let sit for 5 minutes.

4. Serve with your favorite toasted bread or over white rice.

Makes 8-10 servings.

Brands may vary by region; substitute a similar product.

Michael Brando

Michael Brando studied culinary arts internationally and has achieved Master Chef status. He is now celebrating his 37th professional year in culinary arts and is a gold and silver medal winner in several international culinary competitions. During the past decade, Brando has focused his culinary career in the area of product development for both the food-service and retail marketplace. Throughout that period, he has successfully developed and launched several hundred innovative products.

Chef Brando's Pork Schnitzel with Applewood Smoked Bacon and Sage
SMITHFIELD/FARMER'S ▲

All recipes developed by Michael Brando

1 ½ pounds Smithfield* pork tenderloins, sliced and lightly pounded into eight 3-ounce cutlets

8 fresh sage leaves

8 slices well-cooked Farmer's* Applewood Smoked Thick Bacon

Salt

Freshly ground pepper

1-2 tablespoons all-purpose flour

3 tablespoons olive oil

1 cup chicken stock

2 tablespoons dry vermouth

1. Rinse pork cutlets under cold running water and pat dry.

2. Carefully rinse sage leaves and pat dry.

3. Place 1 sage leaf on each piece of meat. Top with a folded slice of bacon, fold cutlet in half and secure with a toothpick. Season to taste with salt and pepper; dust with flour.

4. Heat olive oil in a frying pan over medium-high heat and sear the meat for 2-3 minutes on each side. Remove meat from the pan and keep warm.

5. Pour chicken stock and vermouth into the pan, scraping the bottom for meat particles. Check seasoning.

6. Pour sauce over meat and serve. Makes 4 servings.

* Brands may vary by region; substitute a similar product.

Smithfield. Smithfield™ Beef Group

   CARANDO Classic Italian

CURLY'S · FARMERS HICKORY BRAND · KIRKLAND Signature

Rib-Stuffed Spoon Bread
CURLY'S ▲

20 canned pineapple
rings, drained

Vegetable cooking spray

Flour

2 8 ¹/₂-ounce boxes corn
bread mix

1 tablespoon *each* finely diced
red, yellow, green
and orange bell pepper

¹/₂ teaspoon Mexican or regular
dried oregano

¹/₂ teaspoon dried cilantro flakes

¹/₄ teaspoon red pepper flakes

1 teaspoon sugar

1 full slab Curly's* fully cooked
pork baby back ribs in
barbecue sauce

3 ounces shredded Mexican
cheese blend

1. Preheat oven to 400°F. Heat grill until smoking hot.

2. Lightly coat 1 side of pineapple rings with cooking spray. Place sprayed
side down on grill and cook until grill marks appear, 1 ¹/₂-2 minutes.
Alternatively, heat a sauté pan over high heat for 2 minutes. Add pineapple
and sear until golden brown, about 2 minutes.

3. Coat a 12-by-9-by-1-inch disposable aluminum baking pan with cooking
spray and dust with flour. Blend corn bread mix. Stir in bell pepper, seasonings
and sugar. Pour into pan.

4. Slice pork into individual ribs. Scrape off excess sauce and reserve.
Insert 10 ribs into batter, spacing evenly and allowing about 1 inch to
extend over pan edge.

5. Bake until corn bread is almost done. Sprinkle with cheese and finish
baking. Let cool slightly.

6. Heat reserved sauce in a saucepan.

7. To serve, place 2 pineapple rings on each plate. Cut spoon bread into
10 squares and place on top of pineapple. Spoon reserved sauce around
plates. Makes 10 servings.

Brands may vary by region; substitute a similar product.

Palermo Pork Loin en Croute
SMITHFIELD/FARMLAND ▲

2 ¹/₄ pounds Farmland*
boneless pork loin

4 thick slices day-old bread,
crusts removed

2 tablespoons minced fresh
herbs: rosemary, sage, etc.

2 tablespoons freshly grated
Parmigiano-Reggiano cheese

¹/₂ cup Smithfield* Real
Crumbled Bacon

1 garlic clove, minced

Salt and pepper to taste

2 egg yolks, lightly beaten

¹/₄ cup olive oil, divided

¹/₃ cup chicken broth

1 tablespoon balsamic vinegar

SAUCE

¹/₄ cup Cabernet Sauvignon

2 tablespoons salted butter

¹/₂ onion, chopped

2 tablespoons thinly sliced garlic

1 14 ¹/₂-ounce can crushed
tomatoes

1 tablespoon chopped
fresh basil

1 tablespoon fresh oregano

1 bay leaf

Salt and freshly ground black
pepper to taste

1. Preheat oven to 350°F. Trim away any visible fat from the meat.

2. Place bread, herbs, cheese, bacon, garlic, and salt and pepper in a food
processor; pulse until finely ground. Add egg yolks and 1 tablespoon olive
oil; mix well. Encase meat with the mixture, pressing it firmly.

3. Put meat in a baking dish with remaining oil, chicken broth and vinegar.
Roast for 90 minutes, or until internal temperature is 145°F. Remove meat
to a platter.

4. To prepare the sauce, deglaze the roasting pan with wine over
medium-high heat. Heat a sauté pan over medium-high heat. Cook butter,
onion and garlic for 2-3 minutes. Add meat drippings/wine and remaining
sauce ingredients. Cook over medium to medium-high heat for 12-15 minutes,
or until reduced by a third.

5. Slice the meat, arrange on a platter and top with sauce. Makes 6-8 servings.

Brands may vary by region; substitute a similar product.

Estouffade de Boeuf
KIRKLAND SIGNATURE/SMITHFIELD ▲

¹/₂ pound lean sliced Kirkland Signature bacon

3 ¹/₂ pounds bottom round of beef, cubed

¹/₂ cup all-purpose flour seasoned with ¹/₄ teaspoon salt and freshly ground pepper to taste

2 shallots or green onions, sliced

2 medium onions, coarsely chopped

2 large carrots, thickly sliced

2 cups dry red wine

¹/₄ cup brandy

2 garlic cloves, crushed

¹/₂ teaspoon fresh thyme leaves

1 bay leaf, crumbled

1 tablespoon finely chopped fresh parsley

¹/₂ teaspoon salt

1 tablespoon tomato paste

¹/₂ -1 cup beef broth

1. Preheat oven to 300°F.

2. Simmer bacon in water to cover for 10 minutes. Drain, reserve 3 slices and roughly chop remainder. Lay 3 bacon strips in a heavy flameproof casserole just large enough to hold the ingredients.

3. Roll beef cubes in seasoned flour. Layer half of cubes on top of bacon. Cover with half of vegetables and chopped bacon. Repeat layers with remaining beef, vegetables and bacon.

4. Warm wine in a small saucepan. Add brandy, garlic, herbs, salt, pepper to taste and tomato paste. Mix and pour into casserole.

5. Add beef broth until liquid almost covers contents of pan.

6. Bring to a simmer on the stovetop. Cover with foil and a lid; cook in the oven for 3 hours, or until meat is tender.

7. Skim off fat, season to taste and serve. Makes 8 servings.

Diavolino Sandwich ("Little Devil")
KIRKLAND SIGNATURE/CARANDO ▲

1 piece flatbread, or 1 tortilla

1 ³/₄ ounces sliced Carando* pepperoni

1 ³/₄ ounces Kirkland Signature/Carando* spiral-sliced ham

2 ounces sliced provolone cheese

1 ¹/₂ ounces pimiento-stuffed green olives, finely chopped

3 slices fresh tomato

2 basil leaves, thinly sliced

ROMESCO SAUCE

1 head of garlic

2 tablespoons plus ¹/₃ cup extra-virgin olive oil

1 ³/₄ pounds ripe tomatoes, halved and cored

¹/₄ cup toasted blanched almonds

¹/₄ cup toasted peeled hazelnuts

1 dried ancho chile, seeded

1 teaspoon coarse salt

4 tablespoons red wine vinegar

1 slice stale white bread, torn, if needed for body

Salt and pepper

1. Preheat oven to 350°F.

2. To prepare Romesco Sauce, cut top ¹/₄ inch off garlic. Place on a sheet of foil with cut side up. Drizzle with 1 tablespoon olive oil. Wrap loosely and bake for 25-30 minutes, or until lightly golden and soft to the touch. Let cool; squeeze to remove garlic cloves from skin.

3. Place tomatoes in a pan, drizzle with 1 tablespoon olive oil; bake for 20 minutes, or until tender.

4. Place garlic, tomatoes, remaining oil and all other sauce ingredients in a food processor and puree. Add salt and pepper to taste.

5. Spread about ¹/₃ cup sauce evenly on bread, leaving ¹/₂ inch around edges uncovered. Layer meats and cheese on bread. Top with olives and tomato. Sprinkle with basil.

6. Warm in the oven. Makes 1 serving.

Tip: This can be prepared as an open-faced sandwich or rolled like a wrap, using foil to maintain its shape.

Brands may vary by region; substitute a similar product.

Mario Batali

Mario Batali shares his passion for the authentic spirit of Italian food through his restaurants, food and wine shops, cookbooks, television shows and products. His latest cookbook is Mario Tailgates NASCAR Style (The Sporting News, *2006, available at costco.com). Batali's mantra is "Al tavolo non s'invecchia mai—at the table, one never gets old."*

Penne with Cauliflower
KIRKLAND SIGNATURE/GAROFALO ◄
Recipe developed by Mario Batali

1/2 cup Kirkland Signature extra-virgin olive oil
1 garlic clove, crushed
2 pounds tomatoes, peeled, seeded and chopped, or 4 cups
    plum tomatoes, drained and chopped
1 head cauliflower, broken into florets
2 tablespoons salt
1 pound Garofalo* penne
1/2 cup finely chopped fresh Italian parsley
Freshly ground black pepper
1/2 cup freshly grated Kirkland Signature Parmigiano Reggiano
    or pecorino cheese

1. In a 12- to 14-inch sauté pan, heat olive oil over medium heat. Add garlic and cook gently until softened and very light golden brown. Add tomatoes and cook, stirring, until tomatoes begin to break down.
2. Add cauliflower and stir well. Add 1/2 cup very hot water, lower heat to medium and cook for 30 minutes, or until cauliflower is tender.
3. Bring 6 quarts of water to a boil in a large pot and add 2 tablespoons salt. Add penne and cook according to package directions, until tender yet *al dente*.
4. Drain pasta and add to the pan with cauliflower. Stir in parsley and black pepper to taste and toss for 1 minute over high heat.
5. Divide evenly among 6 warmed pasta bowls, top with grated cheese and serve immediately. Makes 6 servings.

* Brands may vary by region; substitute a similar product.

Spaghetti alla Carbonara
KIRKLAND SIGNATURE/GAROFALO ▲
Recipe developed by Mario Batali

2 tablespoons salt
3 tablespoons Kirkland Signature extra-virgin olive oil
8 ounces *guanciale* (cured pork jowl), pancetta or good bacon, diced
1 pound Garofalo* spaghetti
1 1/4 cups freshly grated Kirkland Signature
    Parmigiano Reggiano cheese
4 large eggs, separated
Freshly ground black pepper

1. Bring 6 quarts of water to a boil in a large pot and add 2 tablespoons salt.
2. Combine olive oil and guanciale in a 12- to 14-inch sauté pan set over medium heat, and cook until the guanciale has rendered its fat and is crispy and golden. Remove from the heat and set aside (do not drain the fat).
3. Cook the spaghetti in the boiling water until just *al dente*. Scoop out 1/4 cup of the pasta cooking water and set aside. Drain the pasta.
4. Add the reserved pasta water to the pan with the guanciale, then toss in the pasta and heat, shaking the pan, for 1 minute.
5. Remove from the heat, add 1 cup of the Parmigiano Reggiano, the egg whites and pepper to taste, and toss until thoroughly mixed.
6. Divide the pasta among 4 warmed serving bowls. Make a nest in the center of each serving and gently drop in an egg yolk. Season the egg yolks with more pepper and sprinkle with the remaining 1/4 cup Parmigiano-Reggiano. Serve immediately. Makes 4 servings.

* Brands may vary by region; substitute a similar product.

Neapolitan Meatballs
KIRKLAND SIGNATURE/GAROFALO ▲
Recipe developed by Mario Batali

3 cups day-old bread cut in 1-inch cubes
1 ¹/₄ pounds ground beef
3 large eggs, lightly beaten
3 garlic cloves, minced
³/₄ cup freshly grated Kirkland Signature Pecorino Romano cheese
¹/₄ cup finely chopped Italian parsley
¹/₄ cup pine nuts, toasted
¹/₂ teaspoon salt
¹/₂ teaspoon freshly ground black pepper
¹/₄ cup Kirkland Signature extra-virgin olive oil

1. In a shallow bowl, soak bread cubes in water to cover for 20 minutes. Drain and squeeze out the excess moisture.
2. In a large bowl, combine the bread, ground beef, eggs, garlic, grated cheese, parsley, pine nuts, salt and pepper, and mix with your hands just until blended. With wet hands, form the mixture into 12-15 large meatballs.
3. In a large heavy-bottomed skillet, heat olive oil over high heat until almost smoking. Add the meatballs, working in batches if necessary to avoid overcrowding the pan.
4. Cook the meatballs, turning occasionally, until deep golden brown on all sides, about 10 minutes per batch. Remove from the heat. Makes 12-15 meatballs.
Tip: Serve these delicious meatballs with your favorite Garofalo* pasta.
Brands may vary by region; substitute a similar product.

Salad Caprese
KIRKLAND SIGNATURE/GAROFALO ▲

1 pound Bufala Mozzarella
6-8 ripe tomatoes
Fresh basil leaves, thinly sliced
4 tablespoons Kirkland Signature extra-virgin olive oil
2 tablespoons Kirkland Signature balsamic vinegar of Modena
Salt and pepper
Red pepper flakes (optional)

1. Cut mozzarella and tomatoes into ¹/₄-inch slices. Alternate slices of tomato and mozzarella on a serving plate. Garnish with basil.
2. In a bowl, whisk together olive oil, vinegar, and salt and pepper to taste. Drizzle liberally over the mozzarella and tomatoes.
3. For extra zip, sprinkle with red pepper flakes. Makes 6-8 servings.
Tip: This is a very simple salad, and therefore high-quality ingredients are essential.

Tom Douglas

Tom Douglas is a cookbook author, owner of four restaurants in Seattle, operator of a successful catering company and creator of the Rub with Love line of spice rubs, along with other culinary accomplishments. His third book is I Love Crab Cakes! 50 Recipes for an American Classic *(Morrow Cookbooks, 2006, available at costco.com). See his Web site at www.tomdouglas.com.*

Chicken Pho with
Fresh Herb Salad

Chicken Pho with Fresh Herb Salad
FOSTER FARMS ◄
All recipes developed by Tom Douglas

6 ounces dried rice sticks (thin rice noodles or rice vermicelli)

1 pound Foster Farms* frozen chicken tenderloins, thawed according to package directions

Kosher salt and freshly ground black pepper

2 tablespoons vegetable oil

1 teaspoon minced garlic

1/2 cup peeled and thinly julienned carrot

1/2 cup thinly sliced yellow onion

5 cups chicken stock, homemade or low-sodium canned

2 tablespoons Asian fish sauce

1 tablespoon peeled and grated fresh ginger

Chinese hot chili paste or Sriracha hot chili sauce

HERB SALAD

1 small bunch basil, leaves separated from stems

1 small bunch cilantro, separated into small sprigs

1 1/2 cups mung bean sprouts

1 serrano chile, stemmed, seeded and thinly sliced

1 lime, cut into wedges

1. Cook rice sticks in boiling water until tender, 3-4 minutes. Drain, rinse with cold water, drain again, then divide among 4 large soup bowls.

2. Pat chicken dry with paper towels and season with salt and pepper.

3. Heat oil in a skillet over medium-high heat. Add chicken and sauté, turning to brown both sides, until cooked through, about 10 minutes. During the last couple of minutes, sprinkle with garlic, turning chicken a few times. Transfer chicken to a cutting board and slice.

4. Scatter chicken, carrots and onions over the noodles, dividing evenly among the soup bowls.

5. Put chicken stock in a saucepan and bring to a simmer. Add fish sauce and ginger; simmer for about 5 minutes.

6. To prepare Herb Salad, arrange all ingredients on a platter.

7. To serve, ladle simmering broth into each bowl. Pass salad and hot chili paste for diners to add to their own soup. Makes 4 servings.

Brands may vary by region; substitute a similar product.

Lemon-Oregano Chicken Shish Kebabs with Tzatziki
FOSTER FARMS ▲

1/4 cup olive oil

2 tablespoons fresh lemon juice

1 1/2 teaspoons minced garlic

1 tablespoon chopped fresh oregano

1 teaspoon red pepper flakes

Grated zest of 1 lemon

6 Foster Farms* boneless, skinless chicken thighs, cut in 1 1/2-inch chunks

TZATZIKI

1/2 large cucumber (about 7 ounces)

2 cups plain yogurt

2 tablespoons chopped fresh parsley

2 tablespoons chopped fresh mint

1 tablespoon fresh lemon juice

Kosher salt and freshly ground black pepper

1. Fire up the grill for medium-hot direct heat.

2. Combine olive oil, lemon juice, garlic, oregano, red pepper flakes and lemon zest in a nonreactive pan. Add chicken and marinate in the refrigerator for about 30-45 minutes.

3. Meanwhile, prepare the Tzatziki: Peel and seed cucumber and cut into small dice. In a bowl, combine cucumber, yogurt, parsley, mint and lemon juice. Season to taste with salt and pepper. Set aside, covered and refrigerate.

4. Thread chicken on skewers, shaking off excess marinade. Season generously with salt and pepper. Grill chicken on both sides, turning as needed, until done, about 8 minutes.

5. Remove chicken from the grill and serve with Tzatziki. Makes 4 servings.

Brands may vary by region; substitute a similar product.

Chicken Breasts Stuffed with Dried Fruit and Goat Cheese
FOSTER FARMS ▼

1 tablespoon butter

¹⁄₄ cup finely chopped onion

¹⁄₄ cup pitted and coarsely chopped dates

¹⁄₄ cup coarsely chopped dried apricots

2 tablespoons chopped fresh parsley

2 teaspoons chopped fresh thyme

¹⁄₄ cup crumbled soft fresh goat cheese

Kosher salt and freshly ground black pepper

4 Foster Farms* boneless, skinless chicken breast halves

4 thick bacon slices

2 tablespoons olive oil

1. Preheat oven to 350°F.

2. Heat butter in a small skillet over medium heat. Add onion and cook, stirring, until soft and lightly browned, 5-6 minutes. Set aside to cool.

3. Put dates and apricots in a food processor and pulse until finely chopped. Add parsley, thyme and reserved onions; pulse briefly to combine.

4. Transfer to a small bowl, gently fold in goat cheese and season to taste with salt and pepper.

5. Set chicken breasts on a cutting board. Use a thin, sharp knife to slice a pocket in the thicker side of each chicken breast, not cutting all the way through. Stuff the breasts, spreading the stuffing evenly.

6. Wrap 1 strip of bacon crosswise around each chicken breast. Tie with kitchen string in a few places, being sure to secure the bacon. Season with salt and pepper.

7. Divide oil between 2 large skillets and heat over medium-high heat. When pans are hot, put 2 chicken breasts in each skillet (or use 1 skillet and cook in batches). Sear until nicely browned, 3-4 minutes per side. Transfer chicken to a baking sheet.

8. Bake until chicken is cooked through, 12-15 minutes, turning breasts over about halfway through baking time.

9. Remove chicken from the oven, cut off the string and serve immediately. Makes 4 servings.

Brands may vary by region; substitute a similar product.

Karen MacNeil

Karen MacNeil is the host of the Emmy Award-winning television show Wine, Food & Friends with Karen MacNeil, *as well as the author of a book on pairing wine with food,* Wine, Food & Friends *(Oxmoor House, 2006, available at costco.com) and the multi-award-winning* The Wine Bible *(Workman Publishing, 2000, available at costco.com). She is the long-time wine columnist for* Cooking Light. *See her Web site at www.winefoodandfriends.com.*

Baked Salmon Fillet with Walnut Sauce
MARINE HARVEST ◀
Recipe developed by Karen MacNeil

2 fresh Kirkland Signature* Salmon Fillets (1 ¹/₂-2 pounds each)
3 tablespoons canola oil, plus more for greasing baking dish
1 large white onion, minced
2 large red bell peppers, cored and diced
3 tablespoons Hungarian or Spanish paprika
2 tablespoons tomato paste
1 cup walnut halves
1 teaspoon salt
1 teaspoon freshly ground black pepper
24 ounces sour cream
Juice of 1 lemon
Lemon wedges, for garnish

1. Preheat oven to 400°F. Place salmon in an oiled baking dish.
2. Heat 3 tablespoons oil in a skillet and add onions. Turn the heat to low, cover and cook, stirring occasionally, until onions become soft and pasty (do not brown).
3. Add bell pepper and cook until soft. Stir in paprika and tomato paste and remove from the heat.
4. Briefly toast walnuts, being careful not to burn. Let cool briefly, then add walnuts, salt, pepper and sour cream to onions and bell peppers. Mix well.
5. Spread sauce thickly over the salmon. Drizzle with lemon juice. Bake salmon for about 10 minutes per inch of thickness of fish and sauce (about 15 minutes). Serve with lemon wedges. Makes 6 servings.
Tip: This recipe goes wonderfully with an Alsatian Riesling.
* Brands may vary by region; substitute a similar product.

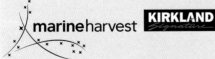

Crispy Salmon Cakes with Lemon-Caper Mayonnaise
MARINE HARVEST ▲

1 tablespoon vegetable oil, divided
¹/₄ cup finely chopped onion
¹/₄ cup finely chopped celery
³/₄ cup crushed fat-free saltine crackers (about 20 crackers), divided
1 tablespoon Dijon mustard
¹/₄ teaspoon freshly ground black pepper
2 7-ounce cans Kirkland Signature* Canned Salmon, drained and flaked
1 large egg, lightly beaten

LEMON-CAPER MAYONNAISE
6 tablespoons fat-free mayonnaise
2 teaspoons capers
¹/₂ teaspoon grated lemon peel
¹/₂ teaspoon lemon juice
¹/₄ teaspoon freshly ground black pepper
¹/₈ teaspoon red pepper flakes

1. Prepare Lemon-Caper Mayonnaise: Combine all ingredients in a small bowl; cover and chill.
2. To prepare the salmon cakes, heat 1 teaspoon oil in a medium nonstick skillet over medium heat. Add onion and celery; sauté for 4 minutes, or until tender.
3. In a medium bowl, combine onion mixture, ¹/₂ cup crackers, mustard, black pepper, salmon and egg.
4. Divide salmon mixture into 4 equal portions, shaping each into a ¹/₂-inch-thick patty. Coat each patty with 1 tablespoon crackers. Cover and chill for 20 minutes.
5. Heat 2 teaspoons oil in a large nonstick skillet over medium heat until hot. Add patties and cook for 5 minutes on each side, or until lightly browned.
6. Serve the salmon cakes with Lemon-Caper Mayonnaise. Makes 4 servings.
Reprinted with permission from *Cooking Light*.
* Brands may vary by region; substitute a similar product.

Chef's Choice I

Spicy Salmon Salad with Red Grapes
MARINE HARVEST ▼
Recipe developed by Karen MacNeil

4 6- to 8-ounce Kirkland
   Signature* frozen salmon
   portions, thawed
2 teaspoons powdered ginger
2 teaspoons garlic powder
1 teaspoon cayenne pepper
4 teaspoons brown sugar
4 teaspoons dark soy sauce
6 tablespoons canola oil
8 cups arugula or mixed baby
   salad greens
2 cups red seedless grapes, halved

VINAIGRETTE
1 cup extra-virgin olive oil
3 tablespoons balsamic vinegar
3 tablespoons tangerine or
   orange juice
½ teaspoon Dijon mustard
1 teaspoon sugar
Salt
Freshly cracked pepper

1. With a sharp chef's knife, cut each salmon portion into four strips, for a total of 16 strips. Lay the strips on a plate and pat with paper towels to dry.

2. In a bowl, combine ginger, garlic powder, cayenne and brown sugar. Add soy sauce and mix well. Using the back of a spoon or a pastry brush, lightly brush the spice mixture onto the salmon strips.

3. Heat canola oil in a large nonstick skillet and sauté salmon strips over medium to medium-high heat for about 3 minutes on each side, or until browned (can be done in 2 batches). Set aside.

4. In a large bowl, toss arugula with grapes and set aside.

5. To prepare the vinaigrette, combine all ingredients in a jar and shake well.

6. To assemble salads, drizzle arugula and grapes with vinaigrette to taste and toss (remainder can be saved for another time). Divide salad among 4 plates. Top each serving with 4 strips of spicy salmon and drizzle with a little of the vinaigrette just before serving to tie the flavors together. Makes 4 servings.

Tip: Try this dish with a bold, spicy Gewurztraminer from California.

* Brands may vary by region; substitute a similar product.

Paula Deen

Teriyaki Shrimp

Paula Deen is a self-made success story who learned the secrets of Southern cooking from her mother and grandmother. Born and raised in Albany, Georgia, Deen moved with her two young sons to Savannah, where she started The Lady & Sons restaurant. She is the author of five cookbooks, including The Lady & Sons Savannah Country Cookbook, The Lady & Sons Just Desserts, Paula Deen & Friends *and* Paula Deen Celebrates! (*some available at costco.com*). *Her Food Network show is* Paula's Home Cooking.

Mazzetta Company, LLC®

Cooking in Style The Costco Way

95

Chef's Choice |

Teriyaki Shrimp
SEAMAZZ ◀

Recipe developed by Paula Deen

1 pound SeaMazz large (U-15) easy-peel shrimp, thawed
Vegetable oil cooking spray

MARINADE
1 tablespoon fresh lime juice
¼ cup dry sherry
¼ cup olive oil
¼ cup prepared teriyaki sauce

1. Peel, rinse and drain shrimp, then place in a resealable plastic bag.
2. To prepare the marinade, combine all ingredients in a glass bowl or measuring cup. Pour over the shrimp, seal the bag and refrigerate for at least 2 hours or overnight.
3. One hour before grilling, start soaking wooden skewers.
4. Preheat grill.
5. When ready to cook, thread shrimp on the skewers, leaving a little space between each shrimp. Place skewers in a grill basket sprayed with cooking spray.
6. Grill over high heat for about 5 minutes on each side, or until just cooked through. Serve hot or cold. Makes 2-3 servings.

Tip: This recipe works wonderfully with larger U-8 or U-6 shrimp, where available. Adjust your cooking times accordingly.

From Paula Deen & Friends (Copyright 2005, Simon & Schuster); used by permission.

Black Pepper Shrimp
SEAMAZZ ▲

Recipe developed by Paula Deen

3 pounds SeaMazz large (U-15) easy-peel shrimp, thawed
8 tablespoons butter
3 tablespoons chopped garlic
4 tablespoons freshly ground pepper

1. Preheat oven to 450°F.
2. Peel, rinse and drain shrimp, then place in a shallow baking pan.
3. In a saucepan, melt butter. Add garlic and sauté for 3-4 minutes. Pour the butter mixture over the shrimp and toss to coat. Pepper shrimp until they are well covered.
4. Bake until pink, approximately 5 minutes, turn, bake a few minutes longer, and pepper again. You must use a heavy hand with the pepper.
5. Serve shrimp with pasta or warm bread and salad. Makes 6 servings.

Tip: This recipe works wonderfully with larger U-8 or U-6 shrimp, where available. Adjust your cooking times accordingly.

Recipe developed by Paula Deen for The Food Network.

Lobster Medallion Salad with Mustard Vinaigrette
SEAMAZZ ▼

2 cups dry white wine

2 cups chicken broth

4 SeaMazz frozen lobster tails, thawed

12 cups mâche or mixed salad greens

4 hard-boiled eggs, sliced

VINAIGRETTE

½ cup Dijon mustard

¼ cup whole-grain mustard

⅓ cup white balsamic vinegar

¼ cup finely chopped green onions

1 tablespoon sugar

1 tablespoon finely chopped fresh oregano

1 tablespoon finely chopped fresh Italian parsley

Salt and pepper to taste

1. Place wine and chicken broth in a saucepan and bring to a boil. Add lobster tails and simmer until opaque in the center, about 10-12 minutes. Drain and let cool. Remove lobster meat from shells and slice into medallions.

2. To prepare the vinaigrette, combine all ingredients in a bowl. Set aside.

3. To assemble salad, place mâche or mixed greens on 4 plates. Top with lobster medallions and sliced eggs. Drizzle 1-2 tablespoons vinaigrette over each salad. Add salt and pepper to taste. Makes 6-8 servings.

Optional: Garnish with assorted sweet peppers.

Recipe created by Linda Carey, culinary specialist.

Bill King

Bill King is vice president of Culinary Development and Training for McCormick & Schmick's Seafood Restaurants, comprising more than 60 restaurants. He has served in the restaurant business for more than 30 years and has been recognized with numerous culinary awards. King was one of the founding members of the Share Our Strength organization's Taste of the Nation fundraiser, now the leading fundraising event for hunger relief in the United States.

Wok-Seared King Crab Legs in Spicy Garlic Sauce
PACIFIC SEAFOOD ◀

All recipes developed by Bill King

3-4 pounds whole king crab legs, split
3 tablespoons toasted sesame oil
4 tablespoons chili paste with garlic
¹/₂ cup chicken stock or broth
¹/₂ cup hoisin sauce
4 tablespoons canola or other vegetable oil
2 tablespoons chopped garlic
4 servings cooked rice, prepared according to package directions
8 sprigs fresh cilantro, for garnish

1. Chop crab legs into smaller sections or leave whole.
2. Combine sesame oil, chili paste, chicken stock and hoisin sauce in a bowl, blend thoroughly and reserve.
3. Heat oil in a wok until very hot. Carefully add crab legs to the wok and toss in the hot oil to coat and heat.
4. Add chopped garlic and the reserved sauce and toss to coat thoroughly.
5. Place rice on 4 plates and top with crab. Pour the sauce over all and garnish with cilantro sprigs. Makes 4 servings.

King Crab Salad with Fresh Citrus and Papaya
PACIFIC SEAFOOD ▲

Juice of ¹/₂ fresh lime
2 teaspoons ground ginger
Pinch of saffron
¹/₂ cup mayonnaise
1 egg yolk*
1 avocado
1 papaya
2 oranges, or other citrus fruit
1-2 heads Bibb or butter lettuce
1 head romaine, chopped
1 pound king crab leg meat

1. Combine lime juice, ginger and saffron.
2. Place mayonnaise in a bowl and mix in seasoned juice and egg yolk to form the dressing.
3. Peel and slice or dice avocado, papaya and oranges.
4. Arrange lettuce leaves and chopped romaine on a plate.
5. Arrange fruit and crab on the lettuce and spoon or drizzle the dressing over all. Makes 4 servings.

If you don't wish to use raw egg yolk, pasteurized egg yolk can be substituted, or just eliminate this ingredient.

Fettuccine Alfredo with King Crab Leg Meat
PACIFIC SEAFOOD ▲

3/4 pound fettuccine
2 tablespoons butter
2 tablespoons chopped garlic
10 button mushrooms, quartered
12 canned artichoke heart halves
1/4 cup dry white wine
1 pint heavy cream
1/2 cup grated Parmesan cheese
1 pound king crab leg meat
2 tablespoons chopped fresh parsley

1. Cook fettuccine according to package directions. Drain and reserve.

2. Heat butter in a large sauté pan over medium heat. Add garlic and sauté for 30 seconds.

3. Add mushrooms and sauté until lightly browned. Add artichokes and toss with mushrooms and garlic.

4. Deglaze the pan with wine for 30 seconds. Add cream and Parmesan; simmer to reduce and thicken for 1-2 minutes.

5. Add crab and reserved fettuccine and toss to thoroughly heat and coat.

6. Divide among 4 pasta bowls or plates and sprinkle with chopped parsley. Makes 4 servings.

Tips for pairing
food & wine

🍷 Pair great with great, humble with humble. Wines and foods of the same "status" have a natural bond. A humble dish like meat loaf doesn't need—doesn't even feel right with—a $60 wine.

🍷 Work with natural flavor affinities. In the same way that coffee and cream just naturally seem to go together, so does, say, a rich salmon fillet and a refreshing white wine.

🍷 Showcase expensive, complex wines with dishes that are utterly simple like, say, a great grilled steak.

🍷 If the wine is delicate, make sure the food is, too. If the food is robust, serve a bold wine.

🍷 The "weight" of the dish and the weight of the wine should always be in harmony. With, for example, a beef stew, opt for a full-bodied red such as Australian shiraz.

🍷 Certain ingredients—known as "bridges"— can tie the flavors of a wine and a food together. For example, adding goat cheese to a salad makes that salad a better match for sauvignon blanc because goat cheese and sauvignon blanc share similar tangy flavors. Adding black peppercorns to a sauce would help bridge that sauce to a wine that is peppery, such as syrah.

🍷 All things considered, wines that are high in acid are generally the easiest to pair with the widest variety of foods. These wines act like a knife, cutting through the flavors of other foods and leaving the palate refreshed and ready for the next bite. Some familiar examples are Riesling, sauvignon blanc and sparkling wines for whites, pinot noir for red.

—Tips courtesy of Karen MacNeil
www.winefoodandfriends.com

Pete Geoghegan

Pete Geoghegan attended the Culinary Institute of America and taught there as a Fellow (assistant instructor). After working in several areas of the food-service industry, Geoghegan brought his extensive and diverse experience to the position of corporate chef, Research and Development, at Cargill Meat Solutions' new Culinary Center of Excellence. In this role, Geoghegan serves as a resource for product, recipe and menu development, product evaluations and demonstrations, cooking and product-handling recommendations, and sensory evaluation.

Roasted Beef Tri-Tip
CARGILL ▲
All recipes developed by Pete Geoghegan

1 2- to 4-pound Morton's of Omaha* Steakhouse Classic Tri-Tip
2 1/2 pounds Yukon Gold potatoes
Kirkland Signature* canola oil
Salt and pepper
2 pounds asparagus, trimmed and peeled
1 tablespoon butter

1. Preheat oven to 425°F.
2. Place beef in a roasting pan fat side up. Roast in the oven for 1 hour, or until internal temperature is 130°F, for medium-rare. Remove from the oven and let rest for 10-15 minutes.

3. Wash potatoes, cut into quarters and place in a bowl. Add oil, salt and pepper to taste, and toss to combine. Place on a sheet pan and roast in the oven for 35-45 minutes, or until golden brown. Potatoes can be roasted with the meat as long as they are not placed too low in the oven, where they may burn.
4. Preheat grill to medium-high.
5. Combine asparagus with canola oil to coat and toss. Grill asparagus for a few minutes, or until tender. Remove from the grill, top with butter and season to taste with salt and pepper.
6. Slice the meat across the grain about 1/8-inch thick and serve with the potatoes and asparagus. Makes 4-6 servings.
Brands may vary by region; substitute a similar product.

Deborah Madison

Deborah Madison's most recent cookbooks are Vegetable Soups *and* Vegetarian Suppers from Deborah Madison's Kitchen. *She is the author of* Vegetarian Cooking for Everyone, The Savory Way *and several other award-winning cookbooks (some available at costco.com). Madison received the M.F.K. Fisher Mid-Career Award from Les Dames d'Escoffier in 1994. See more from Madison at www.randomhouse.com/features/ deborahmadison.*

Summer Salad of Mini Cucumbers, Splendido Tomatoes and Bell Peppers
MASTRONARDI PRODUCE ◄

All recipes developed by Deborah Madison

3 Sunset* mini cucumbers, quartered lengthwise and cut in 3/4-inch chunks

1/2 carton Sunset Splendido* tomatoes, halved

1/2 *each* Sunset* yellow and orange bell peppers, finely diced

2 green onions, including an inch of the firm greens, finely sliced

12 kalamata olives, halved and pitted, plus more for garnish

1/2-1 15-ounce can chickpeas (garbanzo beans), drained

Salt and pepper

VINAIGRETTE

1 tablespoon finely chopped fresh dill

1 tablespoon finely chopped fresh cilantro

1 tablespoon chopped fresh parsley

Finely grated peel of 1 lemon

1 tablespoon lemon juice

3 tablespoons olive oil

GARNISHES (optional)

Crumbled feta cheese

Hard-boiled eggs

Canned or grilled tuna

1. In a roomy bowl, combine cucumbers, tomatoes, peppers, green onions and halved olives. Put chickpeas in a small bowl, cover with cold water and gently swish around with your fingers to loosen the skins. Pour off the water and any loosened skins, gently shake dry and add to the salad. Toss with 3/4 teaspoon salt and plenty of pepper to taste.

2. To prepare the vinaigrette, place herbs, grated lemon peel and juice, and a few pinches of salt in a bowl. Whisk in olive oil.

3. Pour vinaigrette over the salad and toss gently with a wide rubber spatula. Taste for salt. Transfer to a serving bowl.

4. Garnish with olives, and unless you're serving the salad with a meat, fish or chicken dish, add any of the optional garnishes to turn the salad into a complete meal. Makes 4-6 servings.

Tip: To hold the salad for more than 30 minutes before serving, toss the cucumbers with 1/2 teaspoon salt and set in a colander to drain for 30 minutes before adding to the salad. This draws out their water and keeps them nice and crisp.

* Brands may vary by region; substitute a similar product.

Roasted Bell Pepper and Campari Tomato Medley
MASTRONARDI PRODUCE ▲

3 Sunset* bell peppers: 1 each red, yellow and orange

8 Sunset* Campari tomatoes

1 tablespoon minced fresh parsley

1 tablespoon slivered fresh basil

1 garlic clove, minced

2 tablespoons capers

1/2 teaspoon salt

Freshly ground pepper

3 tablespoons extra-virgin olive oil

1. Preheat oven to 400°F. Roast peppers over an open flame, turning every 3-4 minutes, until charred all over. Drop them in a plastic bag, seal and set aside.

2. Slice a small X on the bottom of each tomato. Drop into a pot of boiling water until the skin starts to roll back from the cuts, about 10 seconds, then remove immediately. Slip off the skins, halve the tomatoes crosswise and remove the seeds with your fingers. Slice each half in two and place in a shallow baking dish.

3. Remove as much of the charred skin from the peppers as possible with your hands, then rinse quickly. Don't worry about getting every little bit of black off. Cut off the tops, remove the seeds, then slice the peppers into 1/2-inch-wide strips. Add to the tomatoes, along with the remaining ingredients.

4. Toss everything together until well mingled; cover with foil and bake for 30 minutes. Serve at room temperature. Makes 6-8 servings.

Tip: This roasted medley will keep for 5 days in the refrigerator. It can be used as an appetizer, a sauce for grilled meat, chicken or pasta, or as a filling for a frittata.

* Brands may vary by region; substitute a similar product.

Dr. Connie Guttersen

Dr. Connie Guttersen is a leading nutrition expert and author of the New York Times *best-seller* The Sonoma Diet *(Meredith Books, 2005, available at costco.com) and* The Sonoma Diet Cookbook *(Meredith Books, 2006, available at costco.com). She has devoted her career to developing flavorful approaches to healthy eating and weight reduction. For more information, see her Web site at www.sonomadiet.com.*

Mediterranean Asparagus and Tomato Salad with Pesto Vinaigrette
ALPINE FRESH ◀

All recipes developed by Dr. Connie Guttersen

1 cup cooked white beans, drained
1 cup cooked farro or wheat berries
1 pound Alpine Fresh* asparagus, cut in 1 1/2-inch lengths, blanched
1 cup Alpine Fresh* grape tomatoes, cut in half
1/4 cup kalamata olives, cut in quarters

PESTO VINAIGRETTE
1 cup fresh basil leaves
1 teaspoon finely minced garlic
2 tablespoons toasted pine nuts or walnuts
1/2 cup olive oil
1/4 cup white wine vinegar
1/2 teaspoon salt
1/2 teaspoon freshly ground black pepper

OPTIONAL PROTEIN
8 ounces canned tuna, in large chunks
1 cup bocconcini (bite-size mozzarella balls), cut in half
6 hard-boiled eggs, sliced

1. Prepare Pesto Vinaigrette: Combine basil, garlic, pine nuts and olive oil in a food processor. Pulse until coarsely pureed. Transfer to a bowl and whisk in vinegar, salt and pepper.
2. Place beans, farro or wheat berries, asparagus, tomatoes and olives in a large bowl. Add vinaigrette to taste.
3. Serve with your choice of protein, dressed with a little of the remaining vinaigrette. Makes 6 servings.

* Brands may vary by region; substitute a similar product.

Mango Chutney
ALPINE FRESH ▲

1 pound diced Alpine Fresh* ripe mango
1/3 pound Alpine Fresh* blueberries
1/4 cup diced onion
1/3 cup raisins
1 tablespoon honey
1 tablespoon chopped toasted walnuts
1 tablespoon minced fresh ginger
Dash of minced jalapeño pepper
1 tablespoon cider vinegar
1/2 garlic clove, minced
Juice of 1 lemon
Dash of ground mace
Dash of ground cloves

1. Combine all ingredients in a large saucepan and simmer until mango is soft, about 10 minutes.
2. Strain the solids from the liquid and reduce the liquid over medium heat to a syrup.
3. Combine the solids with the reduced liquid. Cool before serving.
4. Serve with grilled meats and seafood. Makes 5 servings.

* Brands may vary by region; substitute a similar product.

Myra Goodman

Twenty-two years ago, Myra Goodman and her husband, Drew, founded Earthbound Farm in their Carmel Valley, California, backyard. Working closely with the land and its bounty, she developed an appreciation for the benefits of using the freshest ingredients, and she brings that expertise to her culinary endeavors. She is the author of Food to Live By: The Earthbound Farm Organic Cookbook *(Workman Publishing, 2006, available at costco.com).*

California Waldorf Salad
EARTHBOUND FARM ◀
All recipes developed by Myra Goodman

¹/₃ cup nonfat plain yogurt or sour cream
¹/₃ cup mayonnaise
1 teaspoon grated lime zest
2 tablespoons fresh lime juice
2 teaspoons curry powder
¹/₂ teaspoon honey or sugar
¹/₂ cup thinly sliced celery
¹/₂ cup raisins
¹/₂ cup halved seedless grapes
1 unpeeled apple, cored and cut into ¹/₃-inch dice (1 cup)
¹/₂ cup toasted pecans or walnuts
5 ounces Earthbound Farm* Organic Spring Mix or Baby Spinach (about 6 cups)

1. Place yogurt, mayonnaise, grated lime zest, lime juice, curry powder and honey in a small bowl and whisk to combine.

2. Place celery, raisins, grapes, apple and nuts in a large bowl. Add about half of the yogurt dressing and stir to combine.

3. Just before serving, add the spring mix or spinach and toss to combine. Add more dressing if needed. Makes 4 servings.

* Brands may vary by region; substitute a similar product.

Ginger Carrot Soup
EARTHBOUND FARM ▲

2 tablespoons canola oil or olive oil
1 3-inch piece fresh ginger, peeled and coarsely chopped (about ¹/₄ cup)
1 small yellow onion, coarsely chopped (about ³/₄ cup)
4 cups sliced Earthbound Farm* Organic Mini Peeled Carrots (about 1 ¹/₄ pounds)
5 cups vegetable stock or low-sodium vegetable broth
¹/₂ cup fresh orange juice
Pinch of ground nutmeg
Sea salt
Freshly ground pepper
Crème fraîche or sour cream, for garnish

1. Heat oil in a large saucepan over medium heat. Add ginger and onion, and cook, stirring occasionally, until soft and fragrant, about 5 minutes.

2. Add carrots, stock and juice. Raise the heat to medium-high and bring to a boil. Reduce heat to low, cover and simmer until carrots are very tender, about 45 minutes.

3. Puree the soup in the saucepan using an immersion blender. Or let the soup cool a bit, then puree in a blender or food processor and return to the saucepan. If you like a smoother texture, pass the pureed soup through a sieve.

4. Add nutmeg, salt and pepper to taste. If the soup is too thick, thin it with water or stock.

5. To serve chilled, refrigerate the soup until cold, at least 6 hours and up to 5 days. To serve warm, heat slowly over medium-low heat.

6. Garnish each serving with a spoonful of crème fraîche or sour cream. If desired, create a swirl pattern by dragging the tip of a knife or fork through the crème fraîche. Makes 4 servings.

* Brands may vary by region; substitute a similar product.

Sandra Lee

Sandra Lee is an internationally acclaimed lifestylist, a best-selling author and the CEO of Sandra Lee Semi-Homemade® Inc. She has written numerous cookbooks, including the Semi-Home-made *series (some available at costco.com), which led to the debut of* Semi-Homemade Cooking with Sandra Lee *on the Food Network. Lee has been profiled in* Time, Newsweek, Reader's Digest, Woman's Day *and* Gourmet. *See her Web site at www.Semi-Homemade.com.*

Sautéed Bananas over Ice Cream with Oatmeal-Rum Cookies
DOLE ◀

Recipe developed by Sandra Lee

1 17 ¹/₂-ounce package oatmeal cookie mix
¹/₃ cup canola oil
1 large egg, lightly beaten
3 tablespoons dark rum

SAUTÉED BANANAS
¹/₂ stick (¹/₄ cup) butter
4 medium Dole* bananas, underripe, cut diagonally into ¹/₂-inch slices
¹/₄ cup dark rum
3 tablespoons packed brown sugar
¹/₄ teaspoon ground cinnamon

1 pint vanilla bean ice cream

1. Preheat oven to 375°F.
2. In a large bowl, combine oatmeal cookie mix, oil, egg and 3 tablespoons rum. Stir to form a dough. Drop dough by rounded teaspoonfuls onto an ungreased cookie sheet. Bake for 9-11 minutes, or until golden brown. Remove from the cookie sheet and let cool on a wire rack.
3. Meanwhile, to prepare sautéed bananas, melt butter in a large skillet over medium-high heat. Add bananas and cook for 1 minute. Stir in rum, brown sugar and cinnamon. Simmer for 3-4 minutes.
4. Scoop ice cream into 4 dessert dishes. Spoon banana mixture over ice cream. Serve with cookies. Makes 4 servings.
Tip: If you like, bake only as many cookies as you need. The cookie dough can be covered and stored in the refrigerator for 4 to 5 days.
Brands may vary by region; substitute a similar product.

Grilled Chicken Salad with Lemon Poppy Seed Dressing
DOLE ▲

1 cup lemon low-fat yogurt
1 teaspoon poppy seeds
3 boneless, skinless chicken breast halves
6 cups Dole* Classic Iceberg Salad
1 20-ounce can Dole* Pineapple Chunks, drained, or
   1 ¹/₂ cups fresh Dole* Tropical Gold Pineapple cut into chunks
1 cup sliced Dole* fresh strawberries

1. Preheat grill or broiler.
2. Combine yogurt and poppy seeds in a small bowl. Remove 3 tablespoons dressing for the chicken; cover and refrigerate remaining dressing for the salad.
3. Grill or broil chicken for 5-10 minutes on each side, or until no longer pink in the center, brushing occasionally with 3 tablespoons reserved dressing. Discard any remaining dressing. Cut chicken crosswise into ¹/₂-inch-thick slices.
4. Line 3 individual plates with salad blend. Arrange chicken, pineapple and strawberries over the salad. Serve with chilled dressing. If the dressing is too thick, thin with water to desired consistency. Makes 3 servings.
Brands may vary by region; substitute a similar product.

Mark J. Del Priore

Mark J. Del Priore is a graduate of the Culinary Institute of America and has more than 36 years of experience in the restaurant and hospitality industry. He has served as a chef, corporate chef's adviser and general manager in numerous leading establishments, and is currently general manager at St. Andrews Country Club in Boca Raton, Florida. His favorite saying is "I love to eat, but I live to cook."

Stuffed Veal Chops
PLUME DE VEAU ◀

All recipes developed by Mark J. Del Priore

4 Plume De Veau* veal rib chops
1/4 cup white raisins, soaked in 1/4 cup warm sherry for 1/2 hour
1 tablespoon heavy cream (optional)
1 teaspoon minced fresh garlic
1 cup fresh white Italian bread crumbs (crusts removed)
1 egg white
1/2 cup shredded Parmigiano Reggiano cheese
1/4 cup pine nuts, lightly toasted
1 green onion, chopped
1 sprig fresh rosemary leaves, finely chopped
1/4 teaspoon chopped fresh thyme
1/4 teaspoon freshly grated lemon peel
2 tablespoons white truffle oil
Nutmeg, salt and white pepper to taste
1/4 cup olive oil
1/4 cup aged balsamic vinegar
1/4 cup dry white wine
1/2 cup demi-glace
2 tablespoons sweet butter

1. Make a 2-inch incision in the side of each veal chop to create a pocket. Refrigerate.
2. Drain sherry from raisins into a small saucepan. Add cream and garlic, bring to a boil, remove from heat and let cool. In a bowl, combine raisins, bread crumbs, egg white, cheese, nuts, green onion, rosemary, thyme, lemon peel, truffle oil, nutmeg, salt, white pepper and garlic mixture. Stuff veal chops and refrigerate until ready to cook.
3. Preheat oven to 350°F. Season chops with salt and pepper. Heat olive oil in a 12-inch ovenproof skillet over medium-high heat until hot but not smoking. Cook chops until lightly browned. Place chops in the oven for 20 minutes.
4. Remove chops from oven, cover pan and let sit for 10 minutes. Remove chops to a plate. Add vinegar and wine to pan, bring to a boil and cook until reduced to a syrupy consistency. Add demi-glace and swirl in butter.
5. Place veal chops on plates and drizzle with sauce. Makes 4 servings.

* Brands may vary by region; substitute a similar product.

Breaded Veal Scallopini
PLUME DE VEAU ▲

12 1-ounce pieces Plume De Veau* veal scallopini, pounded thin
Salt and white pepper
2 egg whites, lightly beaten
1 cup seasoned dry Italian bread crumbs
1/2 cup plus 1 tablespoon olive oil
1 teaspoon minced garlic
1/4 cup dry white wine, preferably Sauvignon Blanc or Chablis
1/3 cup chicken stock
1/4 cup diced oven-dried tomatoes in oil (drained)
1 cup cooked cannellini beans
2 tablespoons thinly sliced fresh basil
1/4 cup shredded Parmesan cheese, plus more for garnish
2 ounces cold butter, cut into 4 pieces
Freshly ground black pepper

1. Season veal on both sides with salt and pepper. Dip veal into egg whites and then into bread crumbs. Set aside.
2. Heat 1/2 cup olive oil in a 12-inch skillet over medium-high heat until hot but not smoking. Add veal to the skillet in 3 batches and sauté on both sides until light golden. Set aside on a warming plate (do not stack).
3. Remove remaining oil from the pan and add 1 tablespoon olive oil and garlic; sauté briefly until light brown (not dark brown).
4. Remove pan from the heat, add wine, return to the heat and cook until most of the wine has evaporated. Add chicken stock, tomatoes, beans and basil; bring to a quick boil.
5. Lower heat, swirl in 1/4 cup Parmesan and butter, and lightly simmer until thickened. Don't let the mixture come to a rapid boil.
6. Place the bean mixture in 4 bowls and top with veal. Sprinkle with black pepper and additional Parmesan. Makes 4 servings.

* Brands may vary by region; substitute a similar product.

Entrées

Garlic-Stuffed Sirloin
NATIONAL BEEF ◀

1 tablespoon olive oil
¹⁄₄ cup finely chopped fresh garlic
¹⁄₂ cup thinly sliced green onions
¹⁄₄ teaspoon salt
¹⁄₄ teaspoon pepper
**1 3-pound National Beef* Choice boneless top sirloin steak,
    cut 2 inches thick**

1. Preheat grill or barbecue.

2. Heat oil in a small nonstick skillet over low heat. Add garlic and cook for 5 minutes, or until tender, stirring occasionally.

3. Add onions, increase heat to medium-low and continue cooking for 5 minutes, or until onions are crisp-tender, stirring occasionally. Stir in salt and pepper. Remove from the heat and let cool thoroughly.

4. Trim excess fat from steak. Make a horizontal cut through the center of the steak, parallel to the surface, approximately 1 inch from each side. Cut to, but not through, the opposite side. Spoon the cooled stuffing into the pocket, spreading evenly. Secure the opening with wooden picks.

5. Place steak on cooking grid over medium-low coals. Cover grill and cook for 26-32 minutes for rare to medium, turning once. Remove picks.

6. Trim excess fat and carve steak into ¹⁄₂-inch-thick slices. Makes 6 servings.

* Brands may vary by region; substitute a similar product.

Montreal Peppered Steak
McCORMICK ▲

¹⁄₂ cup olive oil
¹⁄₄ cup soy sauce
4 teaspoons McCormick Grill Mates Montreal Steak Seasoning
2 pounds sirloin or strip steaks

1. Mix olive oil, soy sauce and seasoning in a large resealable plastic bag or glass dish. Add steaks and turn to coat well.

2. Refrigerate for 30 minutes, or longer for extra flavor.

3. Preheat grill.

4. Remove steaks from the marinade. Discard any remaining marinade.

5. Grill over medium-high heat for 8-10 minutes per side, or until cooked to taste. Makes 8 servings.

Entrées

Pepper Herb-Crusted Beef Tenderloin
TYSON ▲

2 teaspoons cracked mixed peppercorns
2 garlic cloves, minced
1 teaspoon dried basil leaves, crushed
1 teaspoon dried oregano leaves, crushed
1 whole Choice beef tenderloin, well trimmed (4-5 pounds)
Salt

1. Preheat oven to 425°F.
2. Wash hands. Combine peppercorns, garlic, basil and oregano; press evenly onto the roast.
3. Place roast on a rack in a shallow roasting pan. Insert an ovenproof meat thermometer in thickest part of beef, not resting in fat. Wash hands.
4. Roast meat, uncovered, for 50-60 minutes for medium-rare (internal temperature 140°F) or 60-70 minutes for medium (internal temperature 150°F).
5. Transfer roast to a carving board; tent loosely with aluminum foil. Let stand for 15-20 minutes. (Temperature will continue to rise about 10 degrees.)
6. Carve the roast into thick slices. Season to taste with salt. Makes 4 servings.

Tip: To crack the peppercorns, place them on a cutting board and crush under the bottom of a heavy skillet or by applying pressure to the flat side of a wide knife/cleaver.

Rib Eye Steaks with Marinated Mini Peppers
BIONOVA PRODUCE ▲

10 Vine Sweet Mini Peppers
1 tablespoon lemon juice
$1/2$ cup extra-virgin olive oil
1 tablespoon dried rosemary
Salt and black pepper to taste
4 14-ounce U.S. Choice rib eye steaks

1. As the peppers have very thin skin, don't cook them on an open flame or gas burner, but broil or grill them for about 10 minutes, or until they have darkened or blistered. Cut peppers into very thin slices and place in a container or large cup.
2. Add lemon juice, olive oil, rosemary, and salt and pepper to the peppers and stir to combine. Refrigerate for 2 hours to marinate.
3. Grill the steaks.
4. Arrange the steaks on a tray and pour the marinated peppers over the top. Makes 4 servings.

Meatloaf
LEA & PERRINS ▲

2 pounds ground beef

2 large eggs

1 cup plain dry bread crumbs

$^1/_3$ cup Lea & Perrins Worcestershire Sauce, plus more for topping

$^1/_3$ cup finely chopped onion

$^1/_4$ cup Heinz Tomato Ketchup

1. Preheat oven to 350°F.

2. In a large bowl, combine ground beef, eggs, bread crumbs, $^1/_3$ cup Worcestershire sauce, onion and ketchup.

3. Shape into a loaf in a baking or roasting pan.

4. Sprinkle the top with additional Worcestershire sauce.

5. Bake, uncovered, for 1 hour, or until internal temperature is 160°F.

6. Let stand for 10 minutes before serving. Makes 8 servings.

Tip: For a side dish, try one of the Ore-Ida frozen potato varieties.

Spicy Pork Loin with Corn & Bean Salsa
PRAIRIEFRESH ▲

CORN & BEAN SALSA

2 cups fresh or frozen corn kernels

1 tomato, chopped

1 15-ounce can black beans, drained

$^1/_4$ cup chopped red onion

$^1/_4$ cup chopped red bell pepper

1 4-ounce can chopped green chiles

3 tablespoons finely chopped fresh cilantro

4 tablespoons lime juice

$^1/_2$ teaspoon salt

$^1/_8$ teaspoon ground black pepper

1 teaspoon cayenne pepper

1 teaspoon salt

1 tablespoon dried oregano

1 tablespoon ground black pepper

3- to 4-pound Natural PrairieFresh* Premium Boneless Pork Loin

1. Prepare Corn & Bean Salsa: Combine all ingredients and refrigerate overnight.

2. Preheat oven to 350°F.

3. Combine cayenne pepper, salt, oregano and black pepper; rub mixture over the pork loin.

4. Place pork in a shallow pan and roast for about 1 $^1/_2$ hours, or until internal temperature is 160°F. Let loin rest for 10 minutes before slicing.

5. Serve with Corn & Bean Salsa. Makes 8-10 servings.

* Brands may vary by region; substitute a similar product.

PREMIUM PORK

A product of Seaboard Foods

Mom Tabak's Pork Chops and Sauerkraut
SAGE FRUIT COMPANY ▲

3 bacon slices
6-8 pork chops
1 medium onion, sliced
2 27-ounce cans sauerkraut
2 small potatoes, peeled and cut in 1-inch cubes
2 small Sage Fruit* Granny Smith apples, peeled and
   cut in bite-size pieces
3 tablespoons brown sugar

1. Preheat oven to 300-325°F.
2. Fry bacon in a large skillet over medium heat until crisp; remove from the pan.
3. Brown pork chops in bacon fat. Remove chops to a casserole and keep warm in the oven.
4. Add onion to the pan and brown for about 5 minutes. Add just enough water to loosen particles from the pan.
5. Drain sauerkraut and rinse. Add sauerkraut to the pan, along with potatoes, apples and crumbled bacon. Sprinkle with brown sugar and mix.
6. Add sauerkraut mixture to the casserole, cover and bake until ready to serve—about 1 hour, as long as the pork chops don't dry out. Adjust time and temperature according to the chops' thickness.
7. Serve with your favorite applesauce. Makes 4-6 servings.

Brands may vary by region; substitute a similar product.

Boneless Pork Chops with Apple Cider Glaze
WOLVERINE PACKING ▲

2 boneless pork chops
2 tablespoons olive oil
1/2 teaspoon salt
1/2 teaspoon pepper
1/8 teaspoon granulated garlic
1/8 teaspoon red pepper flakes

APPLE CIDER GLAZE
1/2 cup apple jelly
1/4 cup apple cider
1/8 teaspoon red pepper flakes
1 tablespoon Dijon mustard

1. Prepare a charcoal fire or gas grill.
2. Prepare Apple Cider Glaze: Place apple jelly, cider and red pepper flakes in a saucepan. Bring to a boil and cook until reduced to 1/2 cup. Add mustard and mix well. Keep warm until ready to use.
3. Rub pork chops with olive oil. Sprinkle chops with salt, pepper, garlic and red pepper flakes.
4. Grill chops over a medium-hot fire for 7 minutes per side, or until cooked to taste. Baste chops with Apple Cider Glaze while cooking, and one final time as you take them off the grill. Makes 2 servings.

Pork Chops with Cherry Apple Reduction Sauce
PRIMAVERA ▼

2 tablespoons olive oil
4 pork chops, medium thickness
Salt and pepper
1 shallot, diced
2 garlic cloves, diced
1 Crystal Market* Pink Lady apple, peeled, cored and diced

3 tablespoons white wine
1/2 cup chicken stock
1 tablespoon Dijon mustard
1 pound Prima Frutta* cherries, pitted and diced, plus more for garnish
2 tablespoons butter

1. Heat olive oil in a large frying pan over medium-high heat.

2. Season pork chops with salt and pepper to taste. Add to the pan and brown on both sides; remove and keep warm.

3. In the same pan, sauté shallots and garlic until soft, about 2 minutes. Add apples and wine; sauté for 1 minute.

4. Add chicken stock, mustard, diced cherries and pork to the pan; simmer over medium heat until the cherries are soft and the pork is cooked all the way through.

5. Remove pork and stir butter into the sauce.

6. To serve, drizzle sauce over pork chops. Garnish with cherries on the side. Makes 4 servings.

Brands may vary by region; substitute a similar product.

Entrées I

Cherry Turkey Roll
CHELAN FRESH ▾

1 boneless, skinless turkey breast
    half (about 1 ½ pounds)

3 teaspoons vegetable oil, divided

¼ cup chopped celery

¼ cup chopped water chestnuts

2 tablespoons chopped onion

1 cup coarsely chopped
    Northwest* fresh sweet cherries

1 cup dried coarse fresh
    bread crumbs**

2 teaspoons chopped fresh sage

1 teaspoon chopped fresh rosemary

½ teaspoon salt

¼ teaspoon ground pepper

Paprika

1. Preheat oven to 325°F.

2. Cut turkey breast horizontally toward the thick edge to within ³/4 inch of the edge; do not cut into 2 pieces. The resulting piece should be roughly rectangular in shape. Spread turkey on a sheet of plastic wrap; cover with a second piece of plastic wrap. Pound with a meat mallet to form a rectangular piece ¹/2-inch thick.

3. Heat 2 teaspoons oil in a skillet over medium heat and sauté celery, water chestnuts and onion until crisp-tender. Add cherries, bread crumbs, sage, rosemary, salt and pepper. Mix well.

4. Remove top piece of plastic wrap from turkey. Spread cherry mixture over turkey, leaving 1 inch uncovered along the long edges. Roll tightly and secure with skewers or wooden picks or tie at 2-inch intervals. Brush with remaining oil and sprinkle paprika over entire surface.

5. Bake on a rack in a baking pan for 50-60 minutes, or until internal temperature is 170°F.

6. To serve hot, let stand for 10 minutes before slicing. To serve cold, let cool to room temperature and refrigerate; slice just before serving. Makes 8 servings.

Recipe courtesy of Northwest Cherry Growers.
* Brands may vary by region; substitute a similar product.
** Dry crumbs at 300°F for 5 minutes.

Ginger Grilled Chicken with Tropical Fruit Chutney
CHESTNUT HILL FARMS/ LEGEND PRODUCE ▲

2-inch piece fresh ginger, peeled

4 large garlic cloves

1 teaspoon white peppercorns

1/2 bunch cilantro

2 tablespoons soy sauce

2 tablespoons vegetable oil

1 3-pound chicken, quartered

1 large ripe mango, peeled and diced

1 cup diced cantaloupe

1 medium pineapple, peeled and diced

3 tablespoons sugar

1 teaspoon ground cumin

1/2 cup sweetened grated coconut

1/2 cup roasted peanuts

1 tablespoon minced jalapeño pepper

1. In a food processor, puree ginger, garlic, peppercorns, cilantro, soy sauce and oil.

2. Place puree in a bowl, add chicken and marinate, covered, in the refrigerator for 1 hour.

3. In a saucepan, combine mango, cantaloupe, pineapple, sugar, cumin, coconut, peanuts, jalapeño and 1 cup of water. Bring to a simmer over medium heat and cook until thickened, about 20 minutes.

4. Preheat grill to hot.

5. Grill chicken for 30 minutes, or until cooked through. Serve with tropical fruit chutney. Makes 4 servings.

Recipe courtesy of Chef Allen Susser.

Chicken with Port-Cherry Sauce
GROWER DIRECT/WESTERN SWEET CHERRY ▲

3/4 cup halved and pitted fresh sweet Western Sweet* cherries

2 cups chicken stock or canned low-salt chicken broth

2/3 cup Ruby Port

1 small onion

2 bay leaves

2 fresh thyme sprigs, leaves only

4 6-ounce boneless, skinless chicken breast halves,

pounded to 1/2-inch thickness between sheets of waxed paper

1 teaspoon cornstarch dissolved in 2 teaspoons water

1/4 cup (1/2 stick) butter, cut in 1/2-inch pieces, room temperature

Salt and pepper

1. Place cherries, chicken stock, Port, onion, bay leaves and thyme in a heavy medium saucepan; bring to a boil over high heat. Lower heat and simmer until mixture is reduced to 1/2 cup, about 20 minutes. Discard onion and bay leaves.

2. Meanwhile, heat a large heavy skillet over medium heat. Add chicken breasts and cook for about 6 minutes. Turn chicken over and continue cooking for 8-10 minutes, or until cooked through. Remove from the pan and keep warm.

3. Add cornstarch mixture to the sauce. Bring to a simmer, whisking constantly. Add butter 1 piece at a time, whisking until melted before adding the next piece. Season to taste with salt and pepper.

4. To serve, slice chicken breasts diagonally and fan out on plates. Spoon sauce over the chicken. Makes 4 servings.

* Brands may vary by region; substitute a similar product.

Entrées

Double Orange Chicken
KIRKLAND SIGNATURE/TYSON

Nonstick cooking spray

4 Kirkland Signature/Tyson* Individually Frozen Boneless, Skinless Chicken Breasts, thawed

1/4 cup fresh orange juice

2 tablespoons orange marmalade

1/2 teaspoon grated fresh ginger

1/2 teaspoon salt

1/8 teaspoon ground pepper

2 navel oranges, peeled and sectioned

1. Preheat oven to 425°F.

2. Spray a 13-by-9-inch baking pan with cooking spray. Wash hands. Arrange chicken in the pan. Wash hands.

3. In a small bowl, combine orange juice, marmalade, ginger, salt and pepper; pour over the chicken. Cover the pan tightly with foil; bake for 40 minutes.

4. Baste the chicken with sauce. Bake uncovered for 10 minutes more, or until done (internal temperature 170°F).

5. With a slotted spoon, transfer chicken to a platter. Stir orange sections into the sauce; pour over the chicken. Makes 4 servings.

Serving suggestion: Serve with steamed sugar snap peas and fried rice. Refrigerate leftovers.

Tip: To use frozen breasts, increase cooking time by about one-third.

* Brands may vary by region; substitute a similar product.

Grilled Chicken and Vegetable Kabobs
McCORMICK

1/3 cup olive oil

3 tablespoons white or white wine vinegar

2 tablespoons McCormick* Grill Mates Montreal Chicken Seasoning, plus more to taste

1 pound boneless, skinless chicken breasts, cut in 1 1/2-inch cubes

4 cups assorted fresh vegetable pieces: bell pepper, onion, zucchini, corn on the cob and mushrooms

1. Mix olive oil, vinegar and 2 tablespoons seasoning in a large resealable plastic bag or glass dish. Add chicken and turn to coat well.

2. Refrigerate for 30 minutes, or longer for extra flavor.

3. Preheat grill.

4. Remove chicken from the marinade. Discard any remaining marinade.

5. Alternately thread chicken and vegetables onto skewers. Lightly sprinkle with additional seasoning, if desired.

6. Grill over medium-high heat for 10-15 minutes, or until chicken is cooked through, turning kabobs frequently. Makes 4 servings.

* Brands may vary by region; substitute a similar product.

Stuffed Chicken Breasts Paillard
LA TERRA FINA ▲

4 boneless, skinless chicken breast halves
Salt and pepper
8 ounces La Terra Fina* Chunky Jalapeño Artichoke Dip or
    Artichoke, Parmesan & Garlic Dip
1 tablespoon chopped fresh assorted herbs:
    chives, parsley, thyme, rosemary or any other herb of your choice

1. Preheat oven to 375°F.
2. Pound chicken breasts flat, using the smooth side of a meat mallet, until 1/8-inch thick. Season to taste with salt and pepper.
3. Place approximately 1/4 cup of dip on the bone side of each breast. Roll, secure with toothpicks and place on a baking sheet, seam side down.
4. Sprinkle with fresh herbs.
5. Bake for 15-20 minutes, or until cooked through. Makes 4 servings.

Tip: Serve with seasoned rice and vegetables.

Brands may vary by region; substitute a similar product.

Herbed Chicken with Mushrooms
KIRKLAND SIGNATURE/PERDUE ▲

1 tablespoon olive oil
4 Kirkland Signature/Perdue* Individually Frozen Boneless,
    Skinless Chicken Breasts
8 ounces crimini mushrooms, sliced
1/3 cup chopped shallots
1/3 cup chicken broth
2 tablespoons butter
2 tablespoons chopped fresh herbs: parsley, rosemary or tarragon
Hot cooked long-grain white and wild rice (optional)
Fresh herbs, for garnish (optional)

1. Heat olive oil in a large skillet over medium-high heat. Add frozen breasts, reduce heat to medium, cover and cook for 10-12 minutes. Turn chicken, partially cover and continue cooking for 10 minutes.
2. Add mushrooms and shallots, moving chicken to the outer edges of the pan. Partially cover and cook on medium heat, stirring occasionally, for 5 minutes, or until mushrooms and shallots are golden and softened.
3. Add broth and simmer for 1 minute, stirring and scraping the bottom of the pan.
4. Add butter in small amounts to the skillet, stirring well with each addition. Stir in herbs.
5. To serve, spoon mushroom mixture over the chicken. Accompany with rice and garnish with fresh herbs, if desired. Makes 4 servings.

Brands may vary by region; substitute a similar product.

Provolone, Artichoke and Roasted Red Pepper Stuffed Chicken Breasts
BelGioioso ▲

6 chicken breast halves

6 pieces BelGioioso Sliced Mild Provolone Cheese, diced

3/4 cup canned artichoke hearts, drained and chopped

1/2 cup roasted red peppers, chopped

1 teaspoon kosher salt

1/2 teaspoon cracked black pepper

1/4 teaspoon cayenne pepper

2 tablespoons chopped fresh Italian parsley, plus more for garnish

Kosher salt and cracked black pepper to coat

Olive oil

1. Preheat oven to 400°F.

2. Place chicken breasts on a cutting board and cut a lengthwise pocket along the side.

3. In a medium bowl, combine provolone, artichoke hearts, roasted peppers, 1 teaspoon salt, 1/2 teaspoon cracked pepper, cayenne and 2 tablespoons chopped parsley.

4. Stuff chicken breasts with the filling. Generously sprinkle with salt and pepper.

5. Coat the surface of a large ovenproof sauté pan with olive oil and heat on medium-high. Place chicken breasts in the pan and cook for 3-4 minutes; turn gently and cook for another 3-4 minutes.

6. Transfer the pan to the oven and bake for 15-20 minutes.

7. Transfer chicken and pan juices to plates and garnish with parsley. Makes 6 servings.

BelGioioso®
(bel-joy-oso)

Savory Chicken Stew
DEL MONTE FOODS ▲

4 chicken thighs, skinned

1 tablespoon olive oil

1 cup sliced mushrooms

2 garlic cloves, minced

1 14 1/2-ounce can Del Monte* stewed tomatoes (or S&W* or Contadina* stewed tomatoes)

2 baking potatoes, scrubbed and cubed

1/3 cup dry red wine or beef broth

1 14 1/2-ounce can Del Monte* Fresh Cut or S&W* cut green beans, drained

1. Brown chicken in olive oil in a large skillet over medium-high heat.

2. Push chicken to the side and stir in mushrooms and garlic. Cook and stir for 3 minutes.

3. Add tomatoes, potatoes and wine. Cook, uncovered, over medium heat for 15-20 minutes, or until sauce thickens.

4. Stir in beans, cover and simmer for 5 minutes, or until chicken is done. Makes 4 servings.

Brands may vary by region; substitute a similar product.

Arroz con Pollo y Frijoles
CONAGRA

2 ½ pounds chicken thighs
2 teaspoons garlic salt
1 teaspoon coarsely ground black pepper
Pam Original No-Stick Cooking Spray
1 cup long-grain rice

2 10-ounce cans Rotel* Original Diced Tomatoes & Green Chilies, undrained
1 14 ½-ounce can chicken broth
1 16-ounce can Rosarita* Traditional Refried Beans
½ cup shredded Monterey Jack cheese (2 ounces)

1. Season chicken with garlic salt and pepper.

2. Coat a large skillet with cooking spray. Place chicken, skin side down, in the skillet and brown over medium-high heat for 7 minutes on each side, or until golden brown. Remove chicken from the skillet.

3. Remove all but 2 tablespoons of drippings from the skillet. Add rice and brown over medium heat for about 2 minutes, stirring constantly.

4. Add tomatoes and chicken broth; blend well. Place chicken on top of rice. Bring to a boil.

5. Reduce heat, cover and simmer for 20 minutes, or until rice is tender and chicken is no longer pink. Remove chicken from the skillet and keep warm.

6. Drop beans by tablespoonfuls into the rice; sprinkle with cheese. Heat for 5 minutes, or until beans are hot and cheese has melted. Serve with chicken. Makes 6 servings.

* Brands may vary by region; substitute a similar product.

"In a Heartbeat"
Salmon à la Grapefruit
CAMANCHACA

1 tablespoon olive oil
½ cup finely chopped onions
1 cup fresh grapefruit juice and segments
4 6-ounce portions Camanchaca* skinless, boneless salmon
Fresh grapefruit slices for garnish

1. Heat olive oil in a large nonstick sauté pan over medium heat. Add onions and cook until tender.

2. Add grapefruit juice and segments and salmon to the pan. Cover and simmer over low heat for 6-8 minutes, or until fish is cooked to taste.

3. Serve salmon with sauce, garnished with grapefruit slices. Makes 4 servings.

* Brands may vary by region; substitute a similar product.

Camanchaca
Gourmet Salmon

Salmon Jose Carlos
FJORD SEAFOOD ◄

1 pound Fjord Seafood Atlantic salmon fillet
Olive oil
6 garlic cloves, crushed
1 tablespoon chopped fresh dill

1. Place a sheet of aluminum foil on a baking sheet.

2. Place salmon on the foil. Pour a small amount of olive oil over the salmon—just enough to cover the whole surface.

3. Spread crushed garlic cloves over the top. Sprinkle with dill.

4. Fold aluminum foil over the salmon, seal and refrigerate overnight.

5. Preheat oven to 350°F.

6. Place salmon in the oven, either opening the foil or, if you prefer a moister texture, leaving it sealed. Bake for 15-20 minutes, or until salmon is cooked to taste. Makes 2-3 servings.

Fjord Seafood USA

Baked Salmon in Phyllo
AQUAFARMS ▲

2 large red bell peppers
8 sheets prepared phyllo dough
Cooking spray or olive oil
Aquafarms fresh salmon fillet,
    cut in four 6-ounce portions

Sea salt
Freshly ground black pepper
1 cup crumbled Gorgonzola cheese

1. Roast peppers over an open flame until the outer skin is completely black. Immediately drop peppers into a bowl of ice water. Rub off remaining black skin under running water. Cut peppers in half; remove seeds and tops. Puree peppers in a food processor; set aside.

2. Preheat oven to 375°F.

3. Lay out 4 sheets of phyllo. Spray with cooking spray or brush with olive oil. Top with remaining phyllo sheets.

4. Place salmon portions on phyllo. Lightly season salmon with salt and pepper.

5. Put 2 tablespoons of red pepper puree on top of each fillet. Top with 1/4 cup crumbled Gorgonzola.

6. Roll up salmon in phyllo, folding under outer edges.

7. Coat a baking sheet with cooking spray. Place salmon packets on the baking sheet and spray with cooking spray.

8. Bake for about 25 minutes, or until internal temperature is 160°F. Makes 4 servings.

Recipe created by Willy Ray, Costco Foods Buyer.

AQUA FARMS™

Salmon Carpaccio with Tarragon Oil and Mustard Potatoes
AQUACHILE ▲

12 ounces fresh AquaChile*
salmon loin

3 tablespoons fresh tarragon or
1 tablespoon dried

1/2 cup olive oil

Salt and pepper

MUSTARD POTATOES

6 white potatoes

1 white onion, chopped

1-2 teaspoons Dijon mustard

1/4 cup olive oil

1 teaspoon fresh tarragon,
for garnish

1. Wrap salmon in plastic and place in the freezer until very firm but not frozen. Cut salmon in thin slices. Arrange slices around the edges of a baking sheet, leaving room in the center for the potatoes.

2. Combine 3 tablespoons fresh tarragon and 1/2 cup olive oil in a small saucepan. Cook over low heat for 10 minutes; remove from heat and set aside for about 30 minutes.

3. Prepare Mustard Potatoes: Cut potatoes in cubes and cook in salted water until just tender. Rinse with cold water and drain. In a bowl, mix onion with mustard and olive oil. Stir in potatoes.

4. Preheat oven to 350°F.

5. Sprinkle salmon with tarragon oil and put in the oven for 2 minutes. Season to taste with salt and pepper.

6. Place potatoes in the center of the salmon and garnish with tarragon. Makes 4 servings.

* Brands may vary by region; substitute a similar product.

Salmon Dijonnaise
ALASKA GLACIER SEAFOOD ▲

2 1/2 pounds Alaska Glacier
Seafoods* Organic
skinless salmon
fillets, cut in 6 equal portions

1/4 cup flour

4 tablespoons butter

2 cups sliced mushrooms

1 teaspoon minced garlic

1 cup dry white wine

4 teaspoons Dijon mustard

1 cup heavy cream

1 teaspoon salt

1/2 teaspoon ground pepper

1/4 cup thinly sliced green
onions, for garnish

Cooked brown rice

1. Preheat oven to 350°F.

2. Dust fish with flour.

3. Melt butter in a frying pan over medium-high heat. Cook fish briefly on both sides until very lightly browned but not cooked through. Transfer to a greased 10-by-7-by-2-inch casserole.

4. Add mushrooms and garlic to the frying pan and cook, stirring, until softened. Add wine and mustard. Stir to loosen bits from the pan and pour mixture over fish. Cover and bake for 15-20 minutes, or until fish is cooked to taste.

5. While fish is baking, add cream to the frying pan and boil over medium heat to reduce slightly. Pour in juices from the baked fish. Cook over high heat, stirring, until reduced to 1 1/2 cups. Add salt and pepper.

6. Spoon sauce over salmon, sprinkle with green onions and serve with rice. Makes 6 servings.

Tip: Try this recipe with Alaska Glacier Seafood halibut in place of salmon.

* Brands may vary by region; substitute a similar product.

Stuffed Salmon en Croute
FISH HOUSE FOODS ▼

1 package frozen puff
   pastry, thawed
2 tablespoons flour
1 package Kirkland Signature
   stuffed salmon entrée
1 large egg
2 tablespoons water

2 red bell peppers
1 brown paper bag
4 tablespoons olive oil, divided
Salt and pepper
1 bunch asparagus, trimmed
1 ounce fresh Parmesan shavings
1 lemon, cut in wedges

1. Preheat oven to 400°F.

2. On a lightly floured surface, roll out dough to ⅛-inch thickness. Cut each sheet in half.

3. Place each salmon fillet, stuffing side down, in the center of 1 piece of dough. Wrap dough over fish, trim any excess dough and press edges together to seal. Place seam side down on a cookie sheet. (Use remaining pastry for another purpose.)

4. Beat egg with water and brush evenly over pastry. Bake until golden brown, 25-30 minutes, or according to package directions.

5. Meanwhile, char bell peppers until evenly blackened over an open flame or under a broiler. Enclose in paper bag for 10 minutes. Remove charred skin, stems and seeds; slice into strips. Place pepper strips in a bowl, drizzle with 2 tablespoons olive oil and season to taste with salt and pepper.

6. Cook asparagus in a pot of boiling salted water for 3-6 minutes, or until crisp-tender. Add to the peppers, drizzle with remaining 2 tablespoons olive oil and toss. Check seasoning.

7. Place asparagus spears on each plate, with pepper strips in between. Top with Parmesan.

8. Slice through the center of salmon pastries to expose the stuffing; arrange on plates. Garnish with lemon wedges. Makes 3-4 servings.

Entrées I

Kenneth Gordon May's
World-Famous Salmon Newburg
SMOKI FOODS ▼

1 tablespoon olive oil

1 ½ pounds fresh Kirkland Signature skinless, boneless salmon, or 3 8-ounce pieces Smoki Foods wild Alaska sockeye salmon (skinless)

¼ cup butter

1 12-ounce can evaporated milk

1 egg yolk, beaten

1 tablespoon crushed dried basil leaves or 3 tablespoons chopped fresh basil

1 tablespoon lemon juice

1 teaspoon seasoning salt

8 ounces cream cheese

¼ pound Colby Jack cheese, shredded

¼ pound sharp Cheddar cheese, shredded

2 cups of your favorite rice, uncooked

Paprika

1. Heat oil in a skillet over high heat. Add salmon and cook until browned and just opaque in the center. Cut into bite-size pieces.

2. In a double boiler, combine butter, evaporated milk, egg yolk, basil, lemon juice, seasoning salt, cream cheese, Colby Jack and Cheddar. Cook, stirring constantly, over medium heat until the sauce simmers (do not boil) and is creamy.

3. Add salmon to the simmering sauce.

4. Cook rice according to package directions.

5. To serve, place cooked rice on plates and top with salmon and sauce. Sprinkle with paprika. Makes 6-8 servings.

Variations: Add sautéed sweet onions, sautéed button mushrooms, cooked shrimp or prawns, sautéed scallops or tuna, or all of the above, to the sauce.

Recipe by Chef Mariah May, part owner of Nick's Fishmarket on Oahu and WM The Restaurant on Maui.

SMOKI FOODS

Sweetheart Salmon Fillets
WELCH'S

¹/₄ cup flour
Salt and pepper
4 4- to 6-ounce salmon fillets
3 tablespoons butter or margarine
¹/₂ cup Welch's* 100% grape juice made from Concord grapes
¹/₂ cup chicken broth
¹/₂ teaspoon chopped fresh dill
¹/₄ cup half-and-half
1-2 teaspoons freshly squeezed lemon juice
Lemon slices, for garnish
Parsley, for garnish

1. Combine flour with salt and pepper to taste in a wide, shallow bowl. Dust salmon fillets with flour to coat.

2. Melt butter in a broad skillet. Add salmon and cook over medium-high heat for 5-10 minutes per side, or until fish is opaque or just beginning to flake in the thickest part. Remove to a warm plate.

3. Deglaze pan with grape juice and broth, loosening browned particles. Stir in dill and half-and-half. Cook over medium-high heat just until slightly thickened. Season to taste with salt, pepper and lemon juice.

4. To serve, spoon sauce over salmon fillets. Garnish with lemon slices and parsley. Makes 4 servings.

Recipe courtesy of the New York Wine & Grape Foundation and the National Grape Cooperative.
* Brands may vary by region; substitute a similar product.

Atlantic Salmon and Crab Cakes
AquaGold SEAFOOD

1 pound boneless, skinless fresh Atlantic salmon fillets*, blood line removed, ground in food processor
1 16-ounce can lump crabmeat, drained
1 ¹/₂ cups panko bread crumbs, divided
1 ¹/₂ cups mayonnaise, divided
2 large eggs
1 red bell pepper, cut in ¹/₈-inch dice
1 yellow bell pepper, cut in ¹/₈-inch dice
³/₄ cup chopped cilantro leaves, divided
1 bunch green onions, chopped
Salt and pepper
¹/₂ cup peanut oil
Juice of ¹/₂ lime

1. Preheat oven to 300°F.

2. Place salmon, crab, 1 cup bread crumbs, 1 cup mayonnaise, eggs, bell peppers, ¹/₂ cup cilantro, green onions, and salt and pepper to taste in a large bowl and mix well. Shape into 2-inch patties.

3. Lightly coat both sides of patties with remaining ¹/₂ cup bread crumbs.

4. Heat oil in a frying pan over medium heat. Cook salmon cakes in batches for 2 minutes per side, or until golden brown. Place on a baking sheet in the oven and cook remaining cakes.

5. Serve with Cilantro-Lime Aioli: Place ¹/₂ cup mayonnaise, ¹/₄ cup cilantro and lime juice in a small bowl and mix well. Makes 4-6 servings.

* Brands may vary by region; substitute a similar product.

Grilled Alaskan Halibut Fillets with Blueberry Salsa
AMERICAN FISH & SEAFOOD ▼

2 pounds fresh Alaskan halibut fillets
2 tablespoons extra-virgin olive oil
2 teaspoons kosher salt

BLUEBERRY SALSA

2 cups fresh blueberries, washed
1/2 large red onion, chopped
1/3 cup finely chopped fresh cilantro
2 tablespoons orange juice
1 tablespoon balsamic vinegar
1 teaspoon extra-virgin olive oil
Salt and pepper
1 jalapeño pepper, seeds removed, finely chopped (optional)

1. Prepare Blueberry Salsa: Place 1 cup of the blueberries in a mixing bowl and mash. Stir in remaining blueberries, onion, cilantro, orange juice, vinegar and olive oil. Season to taste with salt and pepper. Add jalapeño pepper for a spicy version. Refrigerate for at least 6 hours and up to 24 hours.

2. Preheat grill.

3. Cut halibut into individual portions. Brush with olive oil and season to taste with salt.

4. Grill halibut over high heat for 5-6 minutes per side, or until fish is opaque in color and flakes easily.

5. Top halibut with Blueberry Salsa and serve immediately. Makes 4 servings.

Ginger Panko-Crusted Flounder with Asparagus and Orange Beurre Blanc
NORTH COAST SEAFOODS ▼

1 cup panko (Japanese bread crumbs)

3 tablespoons ground ginger

2 tablespoons chopped fresh parsley

1 teaspoon kosher salt

2 teaspoons freshly cracked pepper

8 4- to 6-ounce North Coast Seafoods* flounder fillets

Peanut oil

1 pound asparagus, steamed

BEURRE BLANC

1 tablespoon peanut oil

2 tablespoons chopped fresh ginger

2 tablespoons chopped fresh shallot

2 tablespoons chopped fresh garlic

1 cup orange juice

¼ cup chicken broth

1 bunch thyme (about 10 sprigs)

¼ pound butter, cut in 6 pieces

Salt and pepper

1. Combine panko, ground ginger, parsley, salt and pepper in a large shallow bowl. Dredge each flounder fillet in the crumb mixture and set aside.

2. Prepare Beurre Blanc: Heat peanut oil in a saucepan over medium-high heat. Add ginger, shallot and garlic; cook, stirring, for 3-4 minutes. Add juice, chicken broth and thyme; cook over high heat until liquid is reduced to ¼ cup. Strain into a clean pan and keep warm.

3. To cook the fish, heat about 2-3 tablespoons peanut oil in a frying pan over medium-high heat. Place 2 fillets in the pan and cook for 2-3 minutes on each side, making sure they are crisp and lightly browned. Wipe out any burnt crumbs and heat new oil before cooking remaining fillets.

4. To finish the sauce, whisk in butter one piece at a time. Make sure to add the butter slowly so the sauce does not separate. Season to taste with salt and pepper.

5. Arrange 2 fillets and some asparagus on each plate and top with sauce. Makes 4 servings.

Brands may vary by region; substitute a similar product.

Pacific Rim Cod Papillote
TRIDENT SEAFOODS ▲

4 Trident Seafoods Premium Cod frozen fillets

Salt and pepper

1 small carrot, thinly sliced lengthwise

1 red bell pepper, thinly sliced lengthwise

1/2 head Chinese cabbage, shredded

1 1/2 cups fresh bean sprouts

1 bunch green onions, diagonally sliced

1 cup basil leaves

1/2 cup cilantro sprigs

Steamed rice

Sesame seeds

SAUCE

4 tablespoons sesame oil

4 tablespoons teriyaki sauce

2 tablespoons chopped garlic

2 tablespoons grated fresh ginger

1. Preheat oven to 450°F.

2. Place each frozen cod fillet in the center of a 12-inch square of parchment paper or foil. Sprinkle fish with salt and pepper to taste. Add carrots, bell pepper, cabbage, bean sprouts, green onions and basil on top.

3. To prepare the sauce, mix sesame oil, teriyaki sauce, garlic and ginger in a small bowl. Drizzle equally over the fish portions.

4. Seal the packets. Place in a shallow pan and bake for 16-20 minutes.

5. Fold back the parchment paper or foil and sprinkle fish with cilantro sprigs (optional). Serve in packets with a side of steamed rice sprinkled with sesame seeds. Makes 4 servings.

Exotic Tilapia
TROPICAL AQUACULTURE ▲

2 tablespoons olive oil

4 5- to 7-ounce Tropical Aquaculture* tilapia fillets

1/2 tablespoon flour

Salt and pepper

3 tablespoons butter

1 cup fresh pineapple cut in thin matchstick strips

2 tablespoons capers, drained

1. Heat a frying pan over medium-high heat, then add olive oil.

2. Sprinkle both sides of tilapia fillets with flour and salt and pepper to taste. Add to the hot oil and sauté on both sides until golden brown, about 3 minutes per side. Remove to a plate and set aside.

3. Preheat a frying pan over medium heat. Add butter, and when it is hot but not browned, add pineapple and capers. Cook, stirring, for about 1 minute.

4. Spoon pineapple mixture over the fillets and serve. Makes 4 servings.

* Brands may vary by region; substitute a similar product.

Tilapia Four Seasons
REGAL SPRINGS ▼

4 4- to 6-ounce Regal Springs tilapia fillets
Salt and pepper
Paprika
4 tablespoons salted butter
1 medium Vidalia sweet onion, cut in thin strips
1 medium red bell pepper, cut in thin strips
1 medium yellow bell pepper, cut in thin strips
1 medium green bell pepper, cut in thin strips
1 lemon, cut into wedges

1. Preheat oven to 350°F.
2. Place tilapia fillets in a greased baking pan. Add $1/2$ cup water to the pan to keep fillets moist. Season to taste with salt and pepper. Sprinkle with paprika.
3. Bake for 10 minutes, or until white and flaky.
4. Meanwhile, preheat a sauté pan over medium heat. Melt butter, then add onions and sauté for 2 minutes. Add peppers and cook, stirring, until tender.
5. Serve fish with peppers and onions. Garnish with lemon wedges.
Makes 4 servings.

Tilapia Fillets on the Grill
AQUAMERICAS ▼

4 12-by-18-inch sheets aluminum foil
Nonstick cooking spray
4 Aquamericas* tilapia fillets
Olive oil
Salt and pepper
1 lemon, cut into wedges

1. Preheat grill to medium-high.
2. Coat aluminum foil sheets with cooking spray.

3. Place 1 tilapia fillet in the center of each aluminum foil sheet. Drizzle lightly with olive oil and season to taste with salt and pepper.

4. Bring the edges of each foil sheet together to make individual packets. Make sure the packets have a little extra "breathing room."

5. Place packets on the grill, cover and cook for 10-12 minutes.

6. Cut open packets carefully to avoid burns from steam.

7. Garnish with lemon wedges. Makes 4 servings.

Brands may vary by region; substitute a similar product.

aquamericas

Hot and Crunchy Trout
CLEAR SPRINGS ▲

HOT AND CRUNCHY MIX

3 cups corn flakes

2 teaspoons red pepper flakes

3 tablespoons sesame seeds

1/2 cup granulated sugar

MANGO PUREE

3 fresh mangoes, peeled and chopped

1 cup granulated sugar

1 purple onion, chopped

1 jalapeño pepper, seeds removed, minced

2 tablespoons rice wine vinegar

4 Clear Springs* Guaranteed Boneless Rainbow Trout Fillets

Cracked black peppercorns

Sea salt

1/4 cup canola oil

1 cup flour

1 cup buttermilk

1. To prepare Hot and Crunchy Mix, coarsely chop all ingredients in a food processor.

2. To prepare Mango Puree, place all ingredients in a saucepan and simmer for 20 minutes. Puree in a blender. (The mango puree can be prepared in advance and refrigerated overnight.)

3. Season trout on both sides with peppercorns and sea salt.

4. Heat griddle to 350°F and coat with oil.

5. Dredge fish in flour. Dip in buttermilk, then Hot and Crunchy Mix.

6. Remove excess breading and place fish on the griddle, flesh side down. Cook until golden brown, about 4 minutes per side.

7. Serve trout with mango puree. Makes 4 servings.

Tip: Serve on top of saffron rice.

Recipe created by Chef Johnny Carino, star of PBS cooking show Break Me Off a Piece of That.
* Brands may vary by region; substitute a similar product.

Marinated, Broiled or Grilled Rainbow Trout
IDAHO TROUT COMPANY ▲

4 5- to 9-ounce Idaho Trout Company* boneless rainbow trout fillets

4-6 ounces Italian salad dressing

1-2 tablespoons olive oil

Suggested garnishes: lettuce, parsley, lemon wedges, toasted almonds

1. Marinate trout fillets in salad dressing for at least 30 minutes. (You can also marinate them for up to 24 hours in the refrigerator, cutting final preparation time to 10-12 minutes.)

2. Brush a broiler pan with olive oil or line a charcoal or gas grill with aluminum foil.

3. Broil or grill trout on medium-high heat, skin side down, about 4 inches from the heat for 4-6 minutes (for 5- to 6-ounce fillets) or 5-7 minutes (for 7- to 9-ounce fillets), or until the fish flakes easily with a fork.

4. Garnish as desired and serve. Makes 4 servings.

* Brands may vary by region; substitute a similar product.

Herb and Dijon Catfish
DELTA PRIDE ▼

3/4 cup Dijon mustard

1/4 cup dried thyme

3 tablespoons dried dill weed

3 tablespoons lemon juice

1 egg, beaten with fork

1 tablespoon garlic salt

1 tablespoon ground black pepper

4-5 Delta Pride* deep skin catfish fillets

2 cups flour

Salt and pepper

Olive oil

1/4 cup butter

1. In a bowl, combine mustard, thyme, dill weed, lemon juice, egg, garlic salt and 1 tablespoon black pepper until thoroughly mixed. Spread mixture on both sides of catfish fillets.

2. In a shallow bowl, mix flour with salt and pepper to taste. Dredge fillets on both sides in the seasoned flour.

3. Coat a nonstick frying pan with olive oil and heat over medium heat. Add butter right before adding fillets to the pan.

4. Sauté catfish until golden brown, approximately 8-10 minutes. Makes 4-5 servings.

Tip: Fish can also be baked in a 350°F oven for 20-25 minutes.

* Brands may vary by region; substitute a similar product.

Lemon-Dill Sautéed Catfish
DELTA PRIDE ▼

4-5 Delta Pride* deep skin catfish fillets
Salt (preferably sea salt)
Freshly ground pepper
Minced fresh dill or dried dill weed
Lemon juice
1 tablespoon olive oil
½ stick (¼ cup) butter

1. Sprinkle catfish fillets with salt, pepper, dill and lemon juice to taste.

2. Pour olive oil into a skillet and heat over medium heat for 2-3 minutes. Add butter and, as soon as it melts, add fillets.

3. Sauté fillets for 4-6 minutes on each side, or until fish flakes with a fork. If fish seems dry when turning, melt more butter and add with lemon juice. This is important to keep fish moist. Makes 4-5 servings.

Tip: This recipe works well on a grill and in a closed-lid cooker such as a George Foreman. Place fillets in foil to keep all the liquids around the fish.

Brands may vary by region; substitute a similar product.

Fillet of Sole with Grapes and Walnuts
DIVINE FLAVOR ▲

1/2 cup veal or chicken broth
8 fillets of sole
4 sea scallops, halved
8 shrimp, halved
Salt and pepper
Vegetable oil
20 Divine Flavor red or green seedless grapes, halved
16 walnut halves
Juice of 1 lemon
1 teaspoon chopped fresh parsley

1. Heat veal broth in a small saucepan and keep warm.
2. Season the seafood with salt and pepper to taste.
3. Heat oil in a large sauté pan over medium-high heat. Sauté sole for 2-3 minutes per side. Remove from the pan and keep warm.
4. Add scallops and shrimp to the pan and sauté for 30 seconds.
5. Add grapes and walnuts and sauté briefly.
6. Arrange the sole on a serving dish. Cover with the sautéed mixture.
7. Stir lemon juice into the hot veal broth and warm briefly. Pour around the fillets of sole.
8. Garnish with parsley. Makes 8 servings.

Seared Tuna Steaks with Wasabi Sauce
WESTERN UNITED FISH COMPANY ▲

4 fresh Western United Fish Company* ahi tuna steaks (8 ounces, 1 1/2 inches thick)
Kosher salt
Freshly cracked black pepper
4 teaspoons sesame seeds
4 teaspoons peanut oil, divided
4 teaspoons lime juice

1 large sweet onion, sliced
1 large red bell pepper, sliced
2 garlic cloves, minced
1 cup heavy cream
2 teaspoons wasabi powder**
2 teaspoons chopped fresh cilantro

1. Season tuna with salt and pepper; coat with sesame seeds.
2. Heat 3 teaspoons peanut oil in a large sauté pan over medium-high to high heat. Sear tuna for 2 minutes on each side.
3. Remove tuna from the pan. Deglaze pan with lime juice and pour over tuna.
4. In another sauté pan, heat remaining oil over medium to medium-high heat. Add onions, bell pepper and garlic; cook for 2 minutes. Season to taste with salt and pepper.
5. In a small saucepan, combine cream and wasabi. Bring to a boil, lower heat and simmer, stirring occasionally, for 10 minutes, or until it thickens.
6. To serve, cut tuna into 1/4-inch slices. Drizzle with sauce and garnish with cilantro. Serve with sautéed onions and peppers. Makes 4 servings.

* Brands may vary by region; substitute a similar product.
** For a bolder taste, add more wasabi powder.

Your Direct Source

Sea Scallops with Fresh Corn and Tomato Sauce
ATLANTIC CAPES ▼

4 teaspoons olive oil, divided
1 teaspoon finely chopped shallot
1 teaspoon chopped garlic
Kernels from 2 large ears of corn
1 teaspoon finely chopped
  fresh basil
Salt and pepper

½ cup milk
½ pound plum tomatoes, seeded
  and chopped
1 tablespoon chopped fresh parsley
1 tablespoon chopped fresh basil
30 Atlantic Capes sea scallops,
  thawed

1. Heat 2 teaspoons olive oil in a sauté pan over medium heat. Add shallots and garlic; cook until translucent.

2. Add corn, basil, and salt and pepper to taste. Cook until corn is lightly browned, 4-5 minutes. Stir in milk and remove from the heat.

3. Puree the corn mixture in a food processor. Force the puree through a fine sieve into a small saucepan; discard the solids in the sieve. Keep sauce warm over low heat.

4. Place tomatoes, parsley and basil in a bowl and toss. Season to taste with salt and pepper.

5. Pat scallops dry and season to taste with salt and pepper. Heat 2 teaspoons olive oil in a large nonstick skillet over medium heat. Add scallops and sauté, turning once, for 4-5 minutes, or until golden brown.

6. To serve, place about 2 tablespoons of corn sauce in the center of each plate. Top with 5 scallops. Spoon tomatoes over the scallops. Makes 6 servings.

Red Grape Stacks with Seared Sea Scallops
FOUR STAR FRUIT ◀

¹/₄ cup butter

1 ¹/₂ pounds (12) sea scallops, cut in half horizontally

Salt and pepper

36 small fresh spinach leaves

12 pieces Kirkland Signature Parmesan Cracker Bread

GRAPE SAUCE

¹/₄ cup butter

³/₄ cup sliced shallots

¹/₂ tablespoon beef base

4 cups Four Star Fruit red seedless grapes

Sea salt

Freshly ground pepper

¹/₄ cup balsamic vinegar

1 tablespoon lemon juice

1 cup heavy whipping cream

¹/₂ teaspoon dried oregano

1. Heat a large skillet over medium heat. Add butter and then sea scallops. Sear on both sides until golden brown. Season to taste with salt and pepper. Remove from the heat and cover.

2. To prepare grape sauce, in the same pan combine butter, shallots, beef base and grapes. Season to taste with salt and pepper. Cook for 1 minute.

3. Add balsamic vinegar to the grapes and stir to deglaze the pan. Stir in lemon juice, cream and oregano. Reduce heat to low and cook for about 10 minutes, or until the sauce thickens.

4. To assemble each serving, place 3 spinach leaves in the center of a plate. Place 1 piece of cracker bread on top. Place 3 scallops on top and 2 spoonfuls of sauce. Repeat with 2 more layers.

5. Pour sauce over and around each stack. Serve immediately.

Makes 4 servings.

Recipe created by Jean-Yves Mocquet, Costco Foods Assistant General Merchandising Manager.

Pan-Roasted Scallops with Clementines
OUTSPAN ▲

5 Outspan* clementines**

1 pound bay scallops

3 tablespoons olive oil

¹/₂ teaspoon ground allspice

1 19-ounce can chickpeas, drained and rinsed

1 English hothouse cucumber, cut in half lengthwise and flesh scooped out with a melon baller

2 garlic cloves, finely chopped

Salt and freshly ground black pepper

1. Peel and segment 3 of the clementines. Finely grate the peel of the remaining 2 clementines and then juice them.

2. In a large nonmetallic bowl, stir together grated clementine peel, scallops, olive oil and allspice. Cover and refrigerate for 1 hour.

3. In a skillet set over high heat, cook the scallop mixture for 2 minutes.

4. Stir in clementine juice, chickpeas, cucumber balls and garlic; reduce heat to medium and cook for 2 minutes.

5. Stir in clementine segments and cook until just heated through. Season to taste with salt and pepper. Makes 4 servings.

* Brands may vary by region; substitute a similar product.
** Outspan oranges can be substituted.

FISHER CAPESPAN ÒUTSPAN®

Entrées I

"Dark Angels on Horseback" (Glazed Bacon-Wrapped Scallops)
AMERICAN PRIDE SEAFOODS ▼

1/2 cup balsamic vinegar
1/2 cup pure maple syrup
2 teaspoons chopped fresh rosemary or 1 teaspoon dried
8-10 bacon slices
1 pound American Pride U/15 frozen sea scallops, thawed
Fresh rosemary sprigs (optional)

1. Preheat oven to 400°F.
2. Combine vinegar, maple syrup and rosemary in a small saucepan. Bring to a boil, reduce heat and simmer until the glaze is thickened and syrupy, about 10 minutes. Remove pan from the heat and set aside.

3. Cut bacon slices in half. Wrap a half-slice around the circumference of each scallop.
4. Arrange scallops in a baking pan and bake for 8 minutes.
5. Remove scallops from the oven. Drizzle about 1/2 teaspoon of glaze over each scallop, return to the oven and bake for approximately 7-8 minutes.
6. Arrange scallops on a serving plate.
7. Drizzle additional glaze over scallops for decoration, and accent with sprigs of fresh rosemary, if desired. Makes 5-6 servings.

Pan-Roasted King Crab with Garlic Thyme Jus
AQUA STAR ▲

1/2 cup dry white wine
1 tablespoon olive oil
1 tablespoon butter
1 shallot, chopped
1 sprig fresh thyme, leaves removed and chopped
1 teaspoon red pepper flakes
10 garlic cloves, peeled and crushed
1/4 cup canola oil
2 pounds Aqua Star King Crab legs, thawed
1/4 cup chopped fresh parsley

1. Preheat oven to 325°F.

2. In a medium pot, combine wine, olive oil, butter, shallot, thyme leaves, red pepper and garlic. Cook over medium-high heat for 3-4 minutes. Remove from the heat and stir in canola oil.

3. Place thawed crab in an oven-safe dish, cover with sauce and bake for 14-16 minutes, basting every 4-5 minutes with juices.

4. Remove from the oven, place crab in bowls and pour roasting liquid over the top. Garnish with parsley and serve immediately. Makes 4 servings.

When you can't catch your own.™

Wilf's Dungeness Crab Sauté
PACIFIC SEAFOOD ▲

3 tablespoons butter
1 teaspoon minced garlic
1/4 cup nice Chardonnay
1/2 pound Dungeness crab meat
1/2 teaspoon ground white pepper
1/4 cup chopped green onions
Juice of 1/2 lemon
6-8 thin slices of baguette bread
Olive oil
1/4 cup shredded Parmesan cheese

1. In a saucepan, heat butter over medium-high heat. Add garlic, wine and crab. Stir in white pepper, green onions and lemon juice. Cook just until crab mixture is heated through.

2. Meanwhile, preheat broiler.

3. Brush bread slices with olive oil and sprinkle with Parmesan. Place under the broiler until the tops start to brown and bread is crisp.

4. Spoon crab mixture over grilled bread. Serve immediately, with your favorite pasta and fresh vegetable. Makes 2 servings.

PacificSeafood™

Risotto Crab Cakes with Sun-Dried Tomato Basil Pesto
PHILLIPS

2 tablespoons minced onion
1/2 cup diced red bell pepper
5-6 tablespoons olive oil
2 cups prepared risotto, cooled
2 cups panko (Japanese bread crumbs), plus more for coating
4 teaspoons Dijon mustard
2 tablespoons lemon juice
2 tablespoons chopped parsley
1/2 cup mayonnaise
1/2 teaspoon salt
16 ounces Phillips* Crab Meat

PESTO
1/2 cup pine nuts, toasted
1-2 bunches (2 ounces) basil
1/2 teaspoon salt
1/2 teaspoon red pepper flakes
4 tablespoons olive oil
2 tablespoons chopped oil-packed sun-dried tomatoes
2 tablespoons lemon juice
1/2 cup grated Parmesan cheese

1. To prepare pesto, combine all ingredients in a blender or processor and grind to a coarse paste.

2. To prepare crab cakes, sauté onion and bell pepper in 4 tablespoons oil over medium heat until soft but not browned.

3. In a bowl, mix onions and peppers, risotto, panko, mustard, lemon juice, parsley, mayonnaise and salt. Fold in crab.

4. Form crab cakes using 1 cup mixture for each. Coat with panko.

5. Heat 1-2 tablespoons oil in a sauté pan over medium-high heat. Cook crab cakes 2-3 minutes per side, or until golden.

6. Top crab cakes with pesto. Makes 4 servings.

Brands may vary by region; substitute a similar product.

Phillips™

Crab-Stuffed Mushrooms
DOLE MUSHROOMS/ GIORGIO MUSHROOMS

5 large portobello mushrooms or 12 white stuffer mushrooms, cleaned, stems removed
4 tablespoons butter, divided
1 tablespoon *each* finely chopped red, green and yellow bell peppers
2 tablespoons finely chopped shallots
5 tablespoons flour
1 cup evaporated skim milk
1 large egg, beaten
1/2 teaspoon dry mustard
2 teaspoons Worcestershire sauce
1/2 cup mayonnaise
1 pound jumbo lump crabmeat
Dash of paprika, for garnish
Chopped fresh parsley and chives, for garnish

1. Preheat oven to 375°F.

2. Arrange mushrooms on an oiled baking dish.

3. In a skillet, melt 2 tablespoons butter over medium heat and sauté peppers and shallots until tender. Remove from heat and set aside.

4. In a saucepan, melt remaining butter over medium-low heat. Add flour and cook, stirring, for 3-4 minutes; do not brown. Whisk in milk and cook until thickened. Whisk egg into sauce, taking care not to scramble it.

5. Stir in dry mustard, Worcestershire and mayonnaise. Stir in the sautéed vegetables. Gently fold in crab. Spoon mixture into the mushrooms.

6. Bake for 30-35 minutes, or until tender. Sprinkle with paprika, parsley and chives. Makes 5-8 servings.

Dole MUSHROOMS **Giorgio** Fresh Mushrooms

Portuguese-Style Haddock Stew with Littleneck Clams and Mussels
NORTH COAST SEAFOODS ▼

4 tablespoons vegetable oil
1 large Spanish onion, diced
4 garlic cloves, chopped
1 pound chouriço sausage, diced
2 teaspoons ground turmeric
1 pinch saffron
2 tomatoes, diced
8 cups chicken broth
3 Red Bliss potatoes, cut in quarters

24 North Coast Seafoods*
    littleneck clams
4 6-ounce North Coast Seafoods*
    haddock fillets
1 pound North Coast Seafoods*
    P.E.I. mussels
1 small head of kale, stems
    removed, chopped
Kosher salt
Freshly ground black pepper

1. In a large stockpot, heat oil over medium-high heat. Add onion and garlic; cook until onion is soft.

2. Add sausage, turmeric and saffron; cook for 3-5 minutes.

3. Stir in tomatoes, chicken broth and potatoes; cover and simmer until potatoes are tender.

4. Add clams and then gently place haddock in the pot. Cover and cook for about 5 minutes.

5. Add mussels, cover and cook for 5 minutes, or until mussels have opened.

6. Carefully remove haddock and shellfish from the pot and divide among 4 serving bowls.

7. Turn up the heat to high and add kale. Cook until the kale is soft, about 3 minutes. Season to taste with salt and pepper. Pour into the 4 bowls of seafood.

8. Serve with crusty bread and butter. Makes 4 servings.

* Brands may vary by region; substitute a similar product.

Asian Grilled Shrimp Kabobs
HELLMANN'S/BEST FOODS ▲

1 cup Hellmann's or Best Foods Real Mayonnaise
¹/₄ cup apricot preserves
1 tablespoon soy sauce
1 tablespoon Dijon mustard
1 garlic clove, finely chopped
¹/₂ teaspoon ground ginger
8 uncooked prepared shrimp kabobs

1. Preheat grill.
2. In a bowl, combine first 6 ingredients; reserve ¹/₃ cup. Brush kabobs with remaining sauce.
3. Grill kabobs until shrimp turn pink.
4. Serve with reserved sauce. Makes 4 servings.

Variations: Use orange marmalade or mango chutney instead of apricot preserves. Use chicken instead of shrimp kabobs and grill until chicken is thoroughly cooked.

Mediterranean Shrimp Scampi
SEAPAK ▲

1 ¹/₄ cups uncooked orzo pasta (or rice)
¹/₂ package (16 ounces) SeaPak* Shrimp Scampi
1 zucchini, chopped
1 14-ounce can quartered artichoke hearts, well drained
¹/₄ cup chopped sun-dried tomatoes
¹/₂ tablespoon capers
Juice of 1 lemon (about 2 tablespoons)

1. Cook orzo (or rice) according to package directions.
2. Heat a 12-inch skillet** for 1 minute over medium-high heat.
Add frozen shrimp and zucchini to the pan and sauté for 7 minutes, stirring occasionally.
3. Stir in artichokes, sun-dried tomatoes, capers and lemon juice.
Continue cooking, stirring occasionally, for 3-5 minutes, or until shrimp is fully cooked.
4. Serve over orzo (or rice). Makes 4 servings.

Brands may vary by region; substitute a similar product.
**A smaller skillet will require increased cooking time.*

Mini Peppers Stuffed with Shrimp and Plums

1 ½ cups olive oil, divided
5 garlic cloves
16 Divine Flavor* mini peppers, sliced open and seeded
½ onion, chopped
1 green bell pepper, chopped
16 medium shrimp, peeled
8 plums, macerated for 1 hour in sweet white wine, halved, pits removed
8 bacon slices, cut in half
Salt and pepper to taste
1 tablespoon chopped fresh parsley

AIOLI
2 egg yolks
1 pear, cored, peeled and sliced
Juice of ½ orange
1 cup olive oil

1. Heat half of the oil over low heat in a pan, then fry garlic and mini peppers until tender; remove from pan and set aside.

2. Pour the rest of the oil, except for 1 tablespoon, into the pan. Fry onion and bell pepper over low heat until tender.

3. In a separate frying pan, warm 1 tablespoon oil over low heat. Place 1 shrimp inside each plum half, wrap in bacon, close with a toothpick and stuff it inside mini pepper half. Sauté in oil until light brown. Add parsley, then salt and pepper to taste.

4. To prepare aioli sauce, puree garlic in a food processor. Slowly add 1 cup olive oil until emulsified. Add egg yolks and salt.

5. In a saucepan, cook pear and orange juice until tender; mash and stir in garlic mixture. Warm over low heat.

6. Place bell peppers and onions on plates and set stuffed mini peppers on top. Drizzle with aioli sauce. Makes 4-6 servings.

* Brands may vary by region; substitute a similar product.

Red Beans and Rice with Beef Smoked Sausage
JOHN MORRELL/FARMLAND ▲

1 pound dried red beans
1 ½ pounds John Morrell* beef smoked sausage, cut in chunks
½ cup Farmland* bacon cut in large dice
1 large onion, chopped
1 garlic clove, chopped
1 bay leaf
1 teaspoon dried thyme
1 teaspoon ground pepper
½ teaspoon dried sage
1 pinch cayenne pepper
Salt
4 servings freshly cooked rice, prepared per directions

1. Place beans in a Dutch oven and cover generously with water. Let soak for 30 minutes.

2. Sauté chunks of smoked sausage in a frying pan over moderate heat until lightly browned. Drain on paper towels.

3. Add sausage, bacon, onion, garlic, bay leaf, thyme, pepper, sage and cayenne to the beans. Bring to a boil over medium-high heat. Reduce heat to medium-low, cover and simmer for 2 ½ hours, or until the beans are tender, adding water if necessary.

4. Add salt to taste and adjust seasoning.

5. Remove about 3 tablespoons of beans and mash to a paste; return to the Dutch oven and stir. Simmer for 15 more minutes.

6. Serve beans over hot rice. Makes 4 servings.

* Brands may vary by region; substitute a similar product.

Entrées **I**

Cider-Braised Bratwurst with Apples
DOMEX SuperFresh

2 tablespoons olive oil
4 fresh bratwurst (about 1 pound total)
1 large onion, sliced
2 Domex SuperFresh* Fuji or Jonagold apples, cored and cut
   in $1/2$-inch slices
2 teaspoons minced fresh thyme or 1 teaspoon dried
$1/2$ teaspoon salt
$1/4$ teaspoon freshly ground black pepper
1 $1/2$ cups fresh apple cider

1. Heat olive oil in a large skillet over medium heat. Add bratwurst and brown well on all sides, about 5 minutes total. Transfer bratwurst to a plate and set aside.

2. Add onion to the skillet and cook, stirring often, until it begins to brown, 2-3 minutes.

3. Add apple slices, thyme, salt and pepper; stir to mix.

4. Return bratwurst to the skillet, nestling the sausages down into the apple/onion mixture. Pour cider over sausages, loosely cover the skillet with its lid or a piece of foil (so steam can escape) and reduce heat to medium-low. Braise until sausages are cooked through and apples are nearly tender, about 20 minutes.

5. Transfer sausages to a plate and cover with foil to keep warm. Reduce the cooking liquids over medium heat for 2-3 minutes.

6. To serve, arrange bratwurst on individual plates, spoon the apple mixture alongside and drizzle with the cooking liquids. Makes 4 servings.

* Brands may vary by region; substitute a similar product.

Fettuccine with Sausage and Green Olives
PREMIO ▾

2 tablespoons olive oil

6 ounces white mushrooms, sliced

2 garlic cloves, minced

1 1-pound package Premio* sweet Italian sausages, cooked according to package directions and thinly sliced

12-18 large sweet green Italian olives, pitted and sliced

1 pound fettuccine, cooked until *al dente* and drained

2 tablespoons butter

2 tablespoons chopped fresh parsley

Salt and pepper

1 tablespoon grated lemon peel

1. Heat olive oil in a sauté pan over medium heat. Add mushrooms and cook until browned.

2. Add garlic and stir for 30 seconds.

3. Add sausage and olives, and cook, stirring, until well mixed and heated through.

4. Combine sausage mixture with cooked pasta. Add butter and parsley.

5. Check seasoning, adding salt and pepper if necessary.

6. Add grated lemon peel, toss well and serve. Makes 6-8 servings.

* Brands may vary by region; substitute a similar product.

Entrées ▌

No-Boil Classic Lasagna
CLASSICO ▼

1 15-ounce container ricotta cheese
1/2 cup grated Parmesan cheese
2 large eggs
2 32-ounce jars Classico Pasta Sauce (any flavor)
8 ounces lasagna noodles, uncooked
1 pound bulk Italian sausage, cooked and drained
2 cups (8 ounces) shredded mozzarella cheese
Chopped fresh parsley

1. Preheat oven to 350°F.
2. In a medium bowl, combine ricotta cheese, Parmesan cheese and eggs; mix well.
3. In a 13-by-9-inch baking dish, spread 1 cup pasta sauce.
4. Make layers with half each of the uncooked lasagna noodles, ricotta cheese mixture, sausage, remaining pasta sauce and mozzarella.
5. Repeat layering, then sprinkle parsley over the top.
6. Cover tightly with aluminum foil and bake for 1 hour. Uncover and bake for an additional 15 minutes, or until hot and bubbly.
7. Let stand for 15 minutes before serving. Makes 8-10 servings.

Rigatoni Barese
NEW YORK STYLE SAUSAGE ▼

2 tablespoons olive oil
1 pound mild or hot Italian New York Style Sausage*
1 tablespoon minced fresh garlic
Salt and pepper to taste
6 cups torn or coarsely chopped fresh spinach
2 tablespoons chopped fresh basil
1 14 1/2-ounce can stewed tomatoes, coarsely chopped
16 ounces rigatoni pasta
Parmesan cheese, freshly shaved

1. Heat 1 tablespoon olive oil in a large sauté pan over medium heat. Remove casings from sausage and cook, stirring, until crumbled and lightly browned. Drain and set aside in a bowl.

2. Add remaining 1 tablespoon olive oil, garlic, and salt and pepper to taste to the pan and cook until garlic just starts to brown.

3. Stir in spinach and basil, and cook until spinach wilts slightly. Add tomatoes and simmer until spinach is cooked.

4. Add cooked sausage and stir to combine.

5. Meanwhile, cook rigatoni according to package directions. Drain. Add to the sauce and stir to combine well.

6. Garnish with Parmesan cheese. Makes 4 servings.

* Brands may vary by region; substitute a similar product.

Baked Penne and Smoked Sausage
HILLSHIRE FARM ▲

1 pound Hillshire Farm* Polska Smoked Sausage
1 10 ³/₄-ounce can condensed cream of celery soup
2 ¹/₂ cups milk
2 ¹/₂ cups uncooked penne pasta
1 cup frozen peas
1 cup shredded mozzarella cheese
1 ¹/₂ cups canned French fried onions

1. Preheat oven to 375°F.
2. Cut sausage in ¹/₄-inch slices and brown over medium heat in a skillet; drain.
3. Combine soup and milk in a 3-quart casserole. Stir in pasta, sausage, peas, and half of the cheese and onions.
4. Cover tightly with foil and bake for 45 minutes.
5. Uncover and top with remaining cheese and onions. Bake for 3 minutes, or until golden brown. Makes 6 servings.

* Brands may vary by region; substitute a similar product.

White Clam Sauce with Pasta
SEA WATCH ▲

1 51-ounce can Sea Watch* Chopped Sea Clams
3 tablespoons chopped garlic
¹/₂ cup dry white wine
2 tablespoons butter
¹/₂ cup extra-virgin olive oil
¹/₂ cup chopped fresh parsley
1 ¹/₂ pounds pasta, cooked until *al dente* and drained

1. Drain the juice from the can of chopped sea clams into a large sauce pot; set clam meat aside.
2. Add garlic and wine to the clam juice and cook over high heat until reduced by one-third.
3. Lower heat to medium and add butter, olive oil and parsley; simmer for 10 minutes.
4. Add clam meat and cook over low heat for 5 minutes.
5. Pour the sauce over the pasta. Makes 4 servings.

* Brands may vary by region; substitute a similar product.

Spinach and Mozzarella Ravioli with Shrimp and Mushroom Carbonara Sauce
VALLEY FINE FOODS ▲

12 thick bacon slices, cut in 1/4-inch pieces
2 cups yellow onions, cut in 1/2-inch dice
6 garlic cloves, minced
1 pound crimini (brown) mushrooms, sliced
6 egg yolks
3 cups heavy cream
30 shrimp (16/20 count), cooked, peeled and deveined
1/2 cup grated Parmesan cheese
48 Pasta Prima Spinach and Mozzarella Ravioli
1/4 cup olive oil

1. Sauté bacon in a large skillet until crisp; drain grease.
2. Add onions and garlic to the pan and cook over medium heat until tender.
3. Add mushrooms and cook until tender.
4. In a bowl, whisk together egg yolks and cream. Add to the mushroom mixture. Heat, but do not boil, until the sauce thickens.
5. Add cooked shrimp and Parmesan, and mix well.
6. Meanwhile, cook ravioli according to package directions. Drain and toss with olive oil and the Italian herb cheese packet.
7. Pour sauce over the ravioli. Makes 6 servings.

Linguine with Shrimp in Creamy Spinach Artichoke Parmesan Sauce
RESER'S FINE FOODS ▲

2 cups Stonemill Kitchens* Spinach Artichoke Parmesan Dip
2 cups heavy cream
1 teaspoon salt
1/2 teaspoon ground black pepper
1/4 cup olive oil
1 pound shrimp (26/30 count), peeled and deveined
16 ounces linguine, cooked until *al dente* and drained

1. In a bowl, combine dip, heavy cream, salt and pepper. Set aside.
2. Place a 5-quart pot over high heat. Add olive oil and shrimp. Cook, stirring constantly, for 3-5 minutes, or until just cooked through.
3. Add cooked linguine and dip mixture to the pot. Lower heat and cook, stirring frequently, until hot. Serve immediately. Makes 6-8 servings.

* Brands may vary by region; substitute a similar product.

Asparagus Penne Pasta with Shrimp and Sun-Dried Tomatoes
JACOBS MALCOLM & BURTT/NEWSTAR FRESH FOODS/GOURMET TRADING ▲

1 ½ pounds asparagus, trimmed, cut on diagonal into ½-inch pieces
½ cup oil-packed sun-dried tomatoes, drained (reserve 2 tablespoons oil) and chopped
3 large garlic cloves, chopped
½ cup chopped fresh basil, divided
1 ½ pounds peeled raw shrimp
½ teaspoon dried oregano
¼ teaspoon red pepper flakes
1 ¾ cups chicken broth
½ cup dry white wine
2 teaspoons tomato paste
12 ounces penne pasta
½ cup grated Parmesan cheese
¼ cup grated Romano cheese
Salt and pepper

1. In a large skillet over medium heat, sauté asparagus in reserved oil from sun-dried tomatoes for 5 minutes, or until tender. Transfer asparagus to a bowl.

2. Add tomatoes, garlic, ¼ cup basil, shrimp, oregano and pepper flakes to the skillet and sauté until shrimp are just opaque, about 3 minutes. Add to asparagus.

3. Add chicken broth, wine and tomato paste to the skillet and boil until thickened, about 6 minutes.

4. Cook pasta according to package directions. Drain and return to the same pot.

5. Add asparagus and shrimp, sauce, remaining basil and cheese to pasta. Toss over low heat until warmed and sauce coats pasta. Add salt and pepper to taste. Makes 4 servings.

JACOBS MALCOLM & BURTT

Sweet Onion and Salmon with Horseradish Cream Sauce
KEYSTONE ▲

10 ounces orecchiette pasta or other pasta of your choice
6 tablespoons extra-virgin olive oil
2 Keystone* Certified Sweet Onions, cut in large dice
1 cup dry white wine
2 cups heavy cream
3 tablespoons horseradish
24 ounces fresh salmon fillet, poached or grilled
¼ cup grated Parmesan cheese
¼ cup fresh parsley, chopped

1. Cook pasta in boiling salted water until *al dente*. Reserve ¼ cup of the cooking water, then drain pasta and keep warm.

2. Heat olive oil in a heavy skillet over medium heat. Add onions and sauté until lightly caramelized; remove onions from the pan.

3. Deglaze the pan with reserved ¼ cup of pasta water. Add pasta and onions and keep warm.

4. In a saucepan, combine wine and cream; cook over medium-high to high heat until reduced by half. Stir in horseradish.

5. Flake salmon into bite-size pieces.

6. Place pasta and onions on plates. Top with salmon and then sauce. Garnish with Parmesan and parsley. Makes 4 servings.

Compliments of Chef Dave Munson of the Keystone Kitchen.
* Brands may vary by region; substitute a similar product.

Salmon Linguine or Fettuccine
KIRKLAND SIGNATURE/FOPPEN ▲

¹/₂ cup dry white wine
1 cup whipping cream
¹/₄ cup chopped fresh dill
1 teaspoon fresh lemon juice
12 ounces linguine or fettuccine, freshly cooked and drained
4 ounces Kirkland Signature Smoked Salmon, cut in thin strips
4 ounces Foppen* Grilled Salmon, cut in thin strips
Salt and pepper
Lemon wedges

1. Place wine and cream in a large heavy skillet and bring to a boil over high heat. Reduce heat and simmer, whisking occasionally, until the mixture thickens enough to coat a spoon, about 10 minutes. Whisk in dill and lemon juice.

2. Add pasta and toss to coat. Remove skillet from the heat.

3. Add salmon and toss to combine. Season to taste with salt and pepper.

4. Divide pasta among 4 plates. Serve with lemon wedges. Makes 4 servings.

Brands may vary by region; substitute a similar product.

Sugar Snap Peas and Smoked Salmon Penne
SOUTHERN SELECTS ▲

1 pound penne pasta
³/₄ pound Southern Selects* sugar snap peas, halved diagonally
²/₃ cup heavy cream
¹/₂ pound smoked salmon, cut in ¹/₂-inch pieces
3 tablespoons chopped fresh dill
Salt and pepper
¹/₄ cup grated Parmesan cheese

1. Cook pasta in a large pot of boiling salted water for 9 minutes. Add sugar snap peas and continue cooking for 2 minutes. Reserve ¹/₄ cup cooking water. Drain pasta and sugar snap peas in a colander and then return to the pot.

2. Boil cream in a heavy 1-quart saucepan, uncovered, for 2 minutes.

3. Add cream to the pasta and sugar snap peas along with salmon, dill, reserved cooking water, and salt and pepper to taste. Toss to combine.

4. Add Parmesan and toss again. Makes 4 servings.

Brands may vary by region; substitute a similar product.

Classic Tuna Noodle Casserole
CAMPBELL'S ▲

1 can (10 ³/₄ ounce) Campbell's Cream of Mushroom Soup
¹/₂ cup milk
1 cup cooked peas
2 cans (6 ounces each) tuna, rinsed and drained
2 cups hot cooked medium egg noodles
2 tablespoons dry bread crumbs
1 tablespoon butter or margarine, melted

1. Preheat oven to 400°F.
2. Place soup, milk, peas, tuna and noodles in a 1 ¹/₂-quart casserole and stir to combine.
3. Bake for 20 minutes, or until hot. Stir.
4. Mix bread crumbs with butter and sprinkle on top. Bake for 5 more minutes. Makes 4 servings.

Change-of-Pace Chunk Light Tuna Casserole
CHICKEN OF THE SEA ▲

1 10 ³/₄-ounce can condensed cream of mushroom soup
¹/₂ cup light sour cream
¹/₂ pound tri-color rotini pasta, cooked according to package directions and drained
1 10-ounce package frozen chopped broccoli or mixed stir-fry vegetables, thawed
2 tablespoons chopped pimiento
2 tablespoons butter
¹/₂ pound fresh mushrooms, sliced
¹/₂ cup chopped onion
¹/₂ cup chopped celery
2 6-ounce cans Chicken of the Sea Chunk Light Tuna in Spring Water, drained
¹/₂ cup roasted sliced almonds

1. Preheat oven to 350°F.
2. In a bowl, blend soup with sour cream until smooth. Stir in pasta, broccoli and pimiento; set aside.
3. Melt butter in a sauté pan over medium heat and cook mushrooms, onion and celery until tender (about 5 minutes).
4. Mix vegetables into the soup mixture; fold in tuna.
5. Pour tuna mixture into a lightly greased 1 ¹/₂-quart baking dish. Top with almonds.
6. Bake, uncovered, for 25 minutes, or until hot and bubbly. Makes 4-6 servings.

Quick and Creamy Pesto with Spinach and Cheese Ravioli
CIBO NATURALS/ MONTEREY GOURMET FOODS ▼

1 ¼ cups Kirkland Signature by
  Cibo Naturals Basil Pesto

1 ¼ cups plain yogurt

Salt and pepper

1 38-ounce package Monterey
  Pasta Company* Spinach and
  Cheese Ravioli

1 ounce kalamata olives,
  pitted and sliced

3 ounces cherry tomatoes, halved

2 tablespoons toasted pine nuts

Fresh grated Parmesan cheese

1. For the sauce, mix pesto and yogurt in a bowl. Season to taste with salt and pepper. Let stand at room temperature for 1 hour.

2. Cook ravioli according to package directions, drain and divide among 4 plates.

3. Spoon room-temperature sauce over hot ravioli and top with olives, tomatoes, pine nuts and Parmesan. Makes 4-6 servings.

Brands may vary by region; substitute a similar product.

Confetti Pasta Salad with Turkey and Jarlsberg Club Sandwich
JARLSBERG/COTTAGE BAKERY

Costco Deli's turkey and Jarlsberg club sandwich made with Cottage Bakery Whole Grain Bread gives you a gourmet sandwich shop experience without the wait. Jarlsberg cheese is all natural, with a distinctive mellow, nutty flavor and creamy texture. Cottage Bakery Whole Grain Bread is high in fiber and contains many good-for-you grains. Together, they make a sandwich that is perfect for a picnic in the park, a tailgate party or a trip to the beach. Try this easy pasta salad with your sandwich.

1 6 $^1/_2$-ounce jar marinated artichoke hearts, with liquid
$^1/_2$ cup red wine vinegar
2 tablespoons mustard
$^1/_3$ cup chopped sun-dried tomatoes
3 cups cooked tri-color pasta
1 $^1/_2$ cups shredded Jarlsberg or Jarlsberg Lite cheese
1 $^1/_2$ cups thinly sliced celery
1 $^1/_2$ cups chopped green and yellow bell peppers

1. In a large salad bowl, combine artichoke hearts and liquid, vinegar, mustard and sun-dried tomatoes.
2. Add remaining ingredients; toss and serve. Makes 6-8 servings.

Broccoli Salad Entrée
EAT SMART ▲

1 30-ounce package Eat Smart Broccoli Salad
1 12 $^1/_2$-ounce can chunk chicken breast, drained, or 2 cooked whole chicken breasts, cubed
$^1/_4$ cup finely chopped red onion (optional)

1. Place broccoli salad contents in a large bowl and mix according to package directions.
2. Add chicken and red onion. Mix well. Makes 6-8 servings.

Grand Parisian Steak Salad
READY PAC ▼

2 teaspoons vegetable oil
1 pound Choice boneless sirloin steak, cut in thin strips
1 medium green bell pepper, seeded and cut in thin strips
½ medium red onion, thinly sliced
⅔ cup prepared steak marinade (ideally with garlic and cracked black pepper)
1 16-ounce bag Ready Pac Grand Parisian Salad

1. Heat oil in a large nonstick skillet over medium-high heat. Add beef and cook until browned.
2. Add bell pepper and onion, and cook for about 3 minutes, stirring occasionally.
3. Add marinade and cook, stirring occasionally, for 5 minutes, or until vegetables are crisp-tender.
4. Place salad ingredients in a bowl and toss. Divide salad among individual plates and top each serving with steak and vegetables. Makes 4 servings.

Apple Salad with Smoked Chicken and Gorgonzola Cheese
COLUMBIA MARKETING INTERNATIONAL ◀

CHICKEN

4 boneless, skinless chicken
   breast halves

¹/₂ cup brown sugar

¹/₄ cup apple cider

¹/₂ teaspoon liquid smoke

Salt and freshly cracked
   black pepper

DRESSING

¹/₄ cup honey

1 tablespoon Dijon mustard

1 tablespoon minced shallot

1 tablespoon fresh lemon juice

2 tablespoons red wine vinegar

¹/₂ cup extra-virgin olive oil

Salt and freshly cracked
   black pepper

SALAD

16 ounces field greens

2 romaine hearts, chopped

1 red onion, sliced thin

3 CMI* apples of your
   choice, diced

1 cup crumbled Gorgonzola
   cheese, or more to taste

Freshly cracked black pepper

1. Preheat oven to 350°F.

2. To prepare the chicken, place chicken, brown sugar, cider, liquid smoke, and salt and pepper to taste in a bowl and stir to combine. Pour into a roasting pan and bake for 35-40 minutes, or until chicken is cooked. Let cool to room temperature and refrigerate until ready to use.

3. To prepare the dressing, place honey, mustard, shallot, lemon juice and vinegar in a bowl and whisk to combine. Gradually whisk in olive oil. Season to taste with salt and pepper.

4. To make the salad, cut the chicken into bite-size pieces. Place in a salad bowl and add greens, romaine, red onion and apples.

5. Add dressing and toss to coat. Sprinkle with Gorgonzola cheese and cracked pepper to taste. Makes 6 servings.

Recipe courtesy of Chef David Toal of Ravenous Catering, Wenatchee, Washington.
* Brands may vary by region; substitute a similar product.

Grape, Apple and Chicken Salad with Thai Dressing
BLUE SKY FRESH ▲

2 romaine hearts, torn in bite-size pieces

¹/₄ cup thinly sliced green onions

1 Granny Smith apple, cored and sliced thin

¹/₂ cup halved Blue Sky* Thompson seedless grapes

¹/₂ cup halved Blue Sky* Flame seedless grapes

¹/₂ cup halved Blue Sky* black seedless grapes

1 ¹/₂ cups thinly sliced cooked chicken

THAI DRESSING

¹/₂ cup vegetable oil

¹/₄ cup apple cider vinegar

3 tablespoons soy sauce

1 ¹/₂ tablespoons dark sesame oil

¹/₂ tablespoon honey

1 garlic clove, minced

¹/₂ teaspoon peeled, grated fresh ginger

¹/₂ tablespoon sesame seeds, toasted

¹/₄ cup smooth peanut butter

2 teaspoons kosher salt

¹/₂ teaspoon freshly ground black pepper

1. In a large salad bowl, mix romaine, green onions, apple, grapes and chicken.

2. Prepare Thai Dressing: Combine all ingredients in a medium bowl and whisk until well blended.

3. Add dressing to the salad and toss to coat. Makes 6 servings.

* Brands may vary by region; substitute a similar product.

Entrées I

Tropical Chicken and Avocado Salad
AVOCADOS FROM MEXICO ▲

1 fully ripened Mexican* Hass avocado
$^1/_3$ cup olive oil
2 tablespoons lime juice
Salt and freshly ground black pepper
4 cups mixed salad greens, torn in bite-size pieces
2 grilled boneless chicken breast halves (about 8 ounces), sliced
4 slices peeled fresh pineapple
1 large tomato, cut in thin wedges
$^1/_2$ cup thinly sliced red onion

1. Cut avocado in half lengthwise around pit; twist to separate halves. Place the half with the pit on a cutting board; strike the pit with the blade of a sharp knife, twist and pull out pit. With spoon, scoop out flesh and slice.
2. In a small bowl, whisk together olive oil, lime juice, and salt and pepper to taste.
3. Divide greens among 4 serving plates. Top with avocado, chicken, pineapple, tomato and onion. Drizzle with half of dressing.
4. Serve salads with remaining dressing on the side. Makes 4 servings.

* Brands may vary by region; substitute a similar product.

Avocados from Mexico
The world's finest.

Date and Grape Chicken Salad
NATURE'S PARTNER/SunDate ▲

8 cups cubed cooked chicken
2 cups SunDate* Medjool dates, pitted and chopped
2 cups Nature's Partner* red seedless grapes
2 cups water chestnuts, sliced
2 cups diced celery
2 cups sliced nuts
1 $^1/_2$ cups diced pineapple
2 $^1/_2$ cups mayonnaise, or to taste
$^1/_2$ cup chicken broth
1 tablespoon soy sauce
$^1/_2$ teaspoon curry powder, or more to taste
Iceberg lettuce leaves

1. Combine chicken, dates, grapes, water chestnuts, celery, nuts and pineapple in a large bowl.
2. Place mayonnaise, chicken broth, soy sauce and curry powder in another bowl. Stir until well blended.
3. Add just enough dressing to the salad to moisten. Mix gently.
4. Serve in crisp lettuce cups. Makes 6-8 servings.

* Brands may vary by region; substitute a similar product.

Mandarin Orange, Tart Apple and Chicken Salad
ACME FOOD SALES, INC.

1 teaspoon balsamic vinegar
1 tablespoon red wine vinegar
1 tablespoon rice wine vinegar
2 tablespoons extra-virgin olive oil
$^1/_4$ cup sugar (or Splenda)
5-6 ounces mixed salad greens
1 cup diced cooked chicken breast
1 cup Festival* tart apple slices, cut in julienne strips
$^1/_2$ cup sliced toasted almonds
$^1/_2$ cup thinly sliced red onions
1 11-ounce can Festival* mandarin oranges, drained

1. In a bowl, combine vinegars, oil and sugar. Mix until fully emulsified; set aside.
2. In a large salad bowl, combine mixed greens, chicken, apple, toasted almonds and red onions. Toss gently with dressing.
3. Garnish with mandarin oranges. Makes 4-8 servings.

* Brands may vary by region; substitute a similar product.

Entrées I

Vegetable Salad with Citrus Vinaigrette
LITTLE FARM FROZEN FOODS

2 cups Kirkland Signature by NutriVerde Normandy Blend frozen
   vegetable mix, thawed
12 cooked prawns
¹/₄ cup sliced red onion
1 tablespoon chopped fresh cilantro
1 head romaine lettuce, leaves separated
1 tablespoon lemon juice
¹/₄ cup orange juice
1 tablespoon red pepper flakes
5 tablespoons olive oil
Coarse salt and freshly ground pepper

1. In a bowl, combine vegetable mix, prawns, red onion and cilantro.
2. Arrange lettuce leaves on 4 plates. Spoon the vegetable mixture onto the
lettuce leaves.
3. Place lemon and orange juice, red pepper flakes and olive oil in a bowl and
whisk to combine.
4. Pour vinaigrette over the vegetable and prawn mixture. Season to taste
with salt and pepper. Makes 4 servings.

Grapefruit-Crab Salad
DNE WORLD FRUIT

12 lettuce leaves
6 cups torn mixed salad greens
3 Florida grapefruit, peeled
2 medium tomatoes, cut into wedges
2 6-ounce cans crabmeat, drained, flaked and cartilage removed
1 small green bell pepper, sliced into rings
¹/₄ cup reduced-calorie mayonnaise or salad dressing
¹/₄ cup plain fat-free yogurt
1 hard-boiled egg white, chopped
1 tablespoon ketchup
Few drops of hot pepper sauce

1. Line 4 individual plates with 3 lettuce leaves. Top with salad greens.
2. Section grapefruits over a bowl to catch juice; set juice aside. Remove
seeds from sections.
3. Arrange grapefruit sections, tomatoes, crabmeat and pepper rings on
top of greens.
4. For the dressing, in a bowl combine 2 tablespoons of reserved grapefruit
juice, mayonnaise, yogurt, hard-boiled egg white, ketchup and hot pepper
sauce. If the dressing is too thick, stir in additional grapefruit juice, 1 teaspoon
at a time, until it has the desired consistency.
5. Top each salad with some of the dressing. Makes 4 servings.
Recipe from Florida Department of Citrus.

DNE 🌐 Ocean Spray
World Fruit Sales

Spinach and Poached Salmon Salad
METZ FRESH

2 cups dry white wine
  or Champagne

8 cups chicken broth

1 cup balsamic vinegar

1/4 cup lemon juice

1 tablespoon chopped fresh dill
  or 1 teaspoon dried

12 peppercorns

2 bay leaves

4 4-ounce salmon fillets

10 cups Metz Fresh*
  spinach leaves

4 tomatoes, quartered

Salt and freshly ground
  black pepper

Parmesan cheese

DRESSING

1 cup olive oil

4 tablespoons red wine vinegar

1 teaspoon celery salt

1 squeeze fresh lemon juice

2 tablespoons fresh grated
  Parmesan cheese

Salt and pepper to taste

1. In a large saucepan, combine wine, chicken broth, vinegar, lemon juice, dill, peppercorns and bay leaves; bring to a boil.

2. Add salmon, cover and simmer for 10-15 minutes, or until the fish flakes easily. Remove salmon from the pan, let cool to room temperature and then chill thoroughly.

3. Place spinach and tomatoes in a salad bowl.

4. Cut salmon into bite-size pieces and add to the salad. Season to taste with salt and pepper.

5. To prepare dressing, blend all ingredients thoroughly and chill for at least 1 hour. Whisk or shake occasionally while chilling.

6. Add dressing to the salad and toss to coat. Top with shavings of Parmesan. Makes 4 servings.

Brands may vary by region; substitute a similar product.

Dried Cherry Mediterranean Tuna Salad
CHERRY CENTRAL

2 6-ounce cans white tuna in water, drained and flaked

1 cup cut green beans, cooked and drained

3/4 cup Cherry Central* dried tart cherries

1/2 cup shredded carrots

1/2 cup chopped celery

1/2 cup prepared balsamic vinaigrette dressing

1/2 cup crumbled feta cheese

1 tablespoon Dijon mustard

1/4 cup pine nuts, toasted

Salad greens (optional)

1. Combine tuna, green beans, dried cherries, carrots and celery in a medium bowl.

2. Add dressing, cheese and mustard; toss gently until ingredients are lightly coated. Refrigerate, covered, for 2-3 hours to let flavors blend.

3. Sprinkle with pine nuts just before serving. Serve over salad greens, if desired. Makes 4 servings.

Variation: Cherry Central dried blueberries can be substituted for dried cherries to create another interesting flavor.

Brands may vary by region; substitute a similar product.

Cherry Central

Harvest Chicken Sandwich
MILTON'S ▲

1 ¹/₂ cups cooked chicken breast cut in bite-size pieces
2 cups mixed salad greens
1 tablespoon chopped walnuts
1 green apple, cored and chopped
3 tablespoons prepared balsamic vinaigrette
4-6 slices Milton's* Healthy Multi-Grain Plus Bread
2 tablespoons herbed cheese spread

1. Place chicken, mixed greens, walnuts and apple in a bowl.
Add vinaigrette and toss to coat.

2. Toast bread if desired.

3. Spread herbed cheese on 2 slices of bread.

4. Place chicken salad on remaining 2 slices of bread and top with the
other slices. Makes 2-3 servings.

Brands may vary by region; substitute a similar product.

Thomas' Cran-Turkey Muffins
GEORGE WESTON BAKERIES ▲

4 Thomas' Regular English Muffins, split, toasted and buttered
¹/₂ cup prepared cranberry-orange sauce
8 slices cooked turkey
¹/₂ cup shredded Swiss cheese

1. Preheat broiler.

2. Top each muffin half with cranberry-orange sauce, turkey and cheese.

3. Broil 6 inches from the heat for 2 minutes, or until the cheese melts.
Makes 4 servings.

Weston
George Weston Bakeries Inc.

Gourmet Roast Beef Sandwich
LA BREA BAKERY ▼

1/4 cup thinly sliced red onion

4 tablespoons extra-virgin
  olive oil

4 tablespoons balsamic vinegar

1 teaspoon kosher salt

1 teaspoon freshly cracked
  black pepper

1 La Brea Bakery French Demi
  Baguette

3 tablespoons hummus with
  pine nuts

4 slices roast beef

1/2 cup organic salad greens

VINAIGRETTE

1/2 shallot, peeled and
  finely chopped

1/4 cup balsamic vinegar

3/4 cup extra-virgin olive oil

1 1/2 teaspoons finely chopped
  fresh rosemary

1/4 teaspoon kosher salt

1 teaspoon freshly cracked
  black pepper

1. Preheat oven to 350°F.

2. Place red onion in a small bowl and toss with olive oil, vinegar, salt and pepper. Transfer to a baking pan and roast for 10-12 minutes, or until tender. Remove from the oven and reserve.

3. To prepare the vinaigrette, place shallot, vinegar, olive oil, rosemary, salt and pepper in a medium bowl and whisk to combine.

4. Slice baguette in half lengthwise. Spread hummus on the bottom half. Place roast beef slices on the hummus. Top with the roasted red onions.

5. Toss salad greens in vinaigrette to taste and arrange on top of the onions. Reserve remaining vinaigrette for another use.

6. Cover with the top half of the baguette. Makes 1 serving.

Recipe created by Chef Nancy Silverton.

Grilled Portabella Caps
CARDILE BROTHERS

¹/₂ cup extra-virgin olive oil

¹/₄ cup chopped mixed fresh herbs (basil, parsley, thyme, rosemary, oregano, tarragon)

Salt

Freshly ground black pepper

3 pounds Cardile Brothers* Large Portabella Mushroom Caps

6-8 whole wheat buns or a loaf of crusty bread, sliced

¹/₂ pound sliced smoked mozzarella cheese

12-16 green lettuce leaves

2 large ripe tomatoes, sliced

1. Preheat grill.

2. Combine olive oil and herbs in a large bowl. Stir in a dash of salt and pepper to taste.

3. Add mushroom caps to the mixture and stir to coat.

4. Grill mushrooms over medium to medium-high heat, flipping halfway through cooking time, for 4-8 minutes, or until a fork comes out easily.

5. Place grilled mushrooms on buns or bread slices.

6. Top with smoked mozzarella, lettuce and tomatoes.

Makes 6-8 servings.

Brands may vary by region; substitute a similar product.

Simple Summer Salsa
DON MIGUEL MEXICAN FOODS ▲

4 large tomatoes, diced
1 large red onion, diced
2 jalapeño peppers, chopped
3 serrano chiles, chopped
1 yellow bell pepper, seeded and diced
¹/₄ garlic clove, minced
1 bunch cilantro, finely chopped
¹/₂ cup chopped green onions
3 medium tomatillos, chopped
Juice of 1 lemon
1 teaspoon white vinegar
Salt and pepper

1. Combine tomatoes, red onion, peppers, garlic, cilantro, green onions and tomatillos in a large bowl.
2. Add lemon juice, vinegar, and salt and pepper to taste. Mix thoroughly.
3. Chill for 2 hours. Makes 8 servings.

Serving suggestion: Serve with Don Miguel* Flautas or Don Miguel* Mini Tacos.

Brands may vary by region; substitute a similar product.

Broccoli Salad Wrap
EAT SMART ▲

1 30-ounce package Eat Smart Broccoli Salad
9 large flour tortillas
¹/₂ cup prepared teriyaki sauce (optional)

1. Place broccoli salad contents in a large bowl and mix according to package directions.
2. Warm the tortillas.
3. Place 1 cup broccoli salad in the center of each tortilla.
4. Fold up one edge of the tortilla to form the bottom, and roll from one side to the other to create your wrap.
5. Eat as is, or for extra flavor, you can dip your wrap in the teriyaki sauce without adding significant fat/calories. Makes 9 generous wraps.

Savory Chicken Tacos with Caramelized Onions
MISSION ▲

1 tablespoon chili powder
1 teaspoon brown sugar
1/2 teaspoon salt
1 pound boneless, skinless chicken breast halves
Cooking spray
1 tablespoon olive oil

2 garlic cloves, minced
1 1/2 cups thinly sliced onions
1 cup frozen corn
4 Mission* Multi-Grain Soft Taco Size Flour Tortillas or Mission Flour Tortillas
1 cup chopped red bell pepper

1. Preheat oven to 425°F.
2. Combine chili powder, brown sugar and salt; rub evenly over chicken breasts.
3. Place chicken on a broiler pan coated with cooking spray. Bake for 20 minutes, or until cooked through. Remove chicken from the oven; let sit for 5 minutes before slicing.
4. Meanwhile, heat olive oil in a large skillet over medium heat. Add garlic and onions; sauté, stirring frequently, until onions are deep golden, about 25 minutes.
5. Remove onions from the pan and set aside. In the same pan, sauté corn for about 3 minutes, until cooked and slightly browned.
6. Warm tortillas in a skillet over medium heat, 15 seconds on each side (or microwave according to package directions).
7. Fill tortillas with chicken. Top with sautéed onions, corn and chopped bell pepper. Makes 4 servings.

Brands may vary by region; substitute a similar product.

Crispy Fish Tacos
TRIDENT SEAFOODS ▲

8 Trident Seafoods Ultimate Fish Sticks
8 yellow corn taco shells

SPICY SOUR CREAM SAUCE
1 cup sour cream
1 tablespoon diced jalapeño pepper
Juice of 1 lime
2 teaspoons ground cumin
Salt and black pepper to taste

GARNISHES
1/2 cup salsa
2 cups shredded lettuce
1/4 cup thinly sliced red onion
1 cup diced tomato
1/4 cup chopped fresh cilantro
2 tablespoons lime juice
1/2 cup shredded Cheddar cheese
Hot sauce

1. Preheat oven to 475°F.
2. Bake fish sticks on a lightly greased baking sheet for approximately 11-13 minutes.
3. To prepare the sauce, combine all ingredients in a small bowl.
4. Divide the fish sticks among the taco shells.
5. Serve with the sauce and any or all of the garnishes. Makes 4 servings.

Beef Enchiladas and Rice with Black Bean Sauce
KIRKLAND SIGNATURE/EL MONTEREY ▲

1 1/2 cups prepared enchilada sauce
1 cup water
8 Kirkland Signature El Monterey Beef Taquitos
1 5-ounce packet yellow saffron or paella rice mix
1/2 cup frozen diced vegetable mix
1 cup canned black beans, drained
1 cup diced tomatoes with green chiles and onions
1/4 cup Mexican crema or sour cream
1/4 cup crumbled Mexican Cotija or shredded Monterey Jack cheese

1. Combine enchilada sauce and water in a medium sauté pan and bring to a simmer. Add taquitos and simmer, basting regularly, for 3 minutes if thawed or 8 minutes if frozen.

2. Follow the microwave directions on the packet to prepare the rice, adding the mixed vegetables. Set aside.

3. Combine beans and tomatoes in a blender and puree thoroughly. Transfer to a small saucepan and heat to a simmer. Remove from heat, swirl in crema or sour cream and cover to keep warm.

4. Layer the taquitos over the rice and smother with black bean sauce. Garnish with cheese. Makes 4 servings.

Taco Pie
KIRKLAND SIGNATURE ▲

1 prepared 9-inch pie shell
1 pound Kirkland Signature ground beef
Taco seasoning
1 1/2 cups salsa, divided
1 cup sour cream
3 cups shredded Mexican cheese blend
1 1/2 cups crumbled Doritos

1. Preheat oven to 350°F.

2. Prick bottom of pie shell with a fork, then bake for about 10 minutes, or until set.

3. Sauté ground beef until browned, drain and stir in taco seasoning according to package directions. Stir in 1/2 cup salsa.

4. In a bowl, mix remaining 1 cup salsa and sour cream until blended.

5. To assemble, spread 1 cup cooked taco meat in the pie shell. Add 1 cup salsa/sour cream mixture. Sprinkle with 1 1/2 cups cheese. Add remaining meat. Add remaining salsa/sour cream mixture. Sprinkle with 1 1/2 cups cheese. Top with crumbled Doritos.

6. Bake for about 25 minutes, or until crust is golden and internal temperature is 165°F. Makes 4-6 servings.

Recipe created by Willy Ray, Costco Foods Buyer.

  ORLEANS INTERNATIONAL, inc.

Desserts

Amaretto Cheesecake with Madeleine Crust
SUGAR BOWL BAKERY ◀

²/₃ cup Sugar Bowl Bakery* Madeleine pieces, plus
    6 whole cookies for garnish
¹/₄ cup whole raw almonds
3 tablespoons brown sugar
5 tablespoons butter, melted
8 ounces cream cheese, softened
¹/₂ cup granulated sugar
¹/₂ teaspoon almond extract
¹/₄ teaspoon salt
2 large eggs
3 teaspoons amaretto liqueur (optional)
Bittersweet chocolate, for garnish

1. Preheat oven to 350°F.
2. Place ²/₃ cup Madeleine pieces, almonds, brown sugar and butter in a food processor and grind until fine. Pour crumb mixture into an 8-inch springform pan and press firmly onto the bottom and sides.
3. Place cream cheese and granulated sugar in a mixing bowl and beat until smooth. Beat in almond extract and salt.
4. Blend in eggs one at a time, on low speed. Stir in amaretto.
5. Pour batter into the crust.
6. Bake for 35-40 minutes, or until the filling is just set. Let cool to room temperature and then refrigerate until chilled. Makes 12 servings.
Garnish: Take 6 Madeleine cookies and cut diagonally in half. Melt bittersweet chocolate. Dip the bottom of each cookie into melted chocolate, place on a tray lined with foil or waxed paper, and refrigerate until the chocolate hardens. Place a cookie, chocolate side down, on each piece of cheesecake.

Brands may vary by region; substitute a similar product.

Mini Berry Cheesecakes
NATURIPE ▲

12 ounces cream cheese, softened
¹/₃ cup granulated sugar
2 large eggs
1 tablespoon grated lemon peel
2 teaspoons vanilla extract
1 ¹/₂ cups fresh Naturipe* blueberries
1 cup chopped fresh Naturipe* strawberries (¹/₄-inch pieces)
12 foil baking cups
12 gingersnap or vanilla wafer cookies
Berries and fresh mint sprigs, for garnish
Confectioners' sugar (optional)

1. Preheat oven to 350°F.
2. Place cream cheese and sugar in a mixing bowl; beat until smooth. Add eggs, lemon peel and vanilla; beat until smooth. Stir in berries and set aside.
3. Place baking cups in a 12-cup muffin pan.
4. Place a cookie in each baking cup.
5. Divide berry mixture equally among cups.
6. Bake for 25-30 minutes, or until set.
7. Cool to room temperature and then refrigerate until well chilled. Remove from refrigerator 1 hour before serving.
8. To serve, remove cheesecakes from foil cups and place on a plate. Garnish with additional berries and mint sprigs, and dust with confectioners' sugar if desired. Makes 12 servings.
Tip: These cheesecakes can be made 2 days ahead of serving.

Brands may vary by region; substitute a similar product.

Desserts I

Lemon Raspberry Cheesecake
JON DONAIRE DESSERTS ▲

1/2-3/4 cup seedless raspberry preserves, warmed, or raspberry sauce
1 Jon Donaire* Baked New York Cheesecake, thawed (16 slices)
1 cup prepared lemon curd
16 tablespoons sweetened whipped cream or nondairy
    whipped topping
16 fresh raspberries
16 small mint leaves

1. Drizzle each dessert plate with 1-2 teaspoons of raspberry preserves in a pretty zigzag pattern.

2. Carefully place a slice of cheesecake on each raspberry-sauced plate.

3. Spread 1 tablespoon lemon curd over each slice of cheesecake.

4. Spoon 1 tablespoon whipped cream on the edge of each slice.

5. Decorate whipped cream with a fresh raspberry and a mint leaf.
Serve immediately. Makes 16 servings.

Brands may vary by region; substitute a similar product.

Patty's Cherry Jubilee
M&R COMPANY ▲

Pastry dough for 2-crust 9-inch pie
4-5 cups pitted M&R* Rainier cherries
1 cup sugar
Juice of 1/2 lemon
4 tablespoons instant tapioca
1 1/2-2 tablespoons butter, softened
Dash of nutmeg

1. Preheat oven to 375°F.

2. Roll out half of pastry dough and place in a 9-inch pie pan.

3. In a bowl, mix cherries, sugar, lemon juice and tapioca. Pour mixture into the pie shell.

4. Roll out remaining dough, place over filling and seal edges. Spread butter on top.

5. Sprinkle lightly with nutmeg and make 5 slits in the top crust.

6. Bake for 1 hour, or until crust is golden brown. Makes 8 servings.

Brands may vary by region; substitute a similar product.

Peach Pie
I.M. RIPE ▼

Pastry dough for 2-crust 9-inch pie
7 cups peeled and sliced I.M. RIPE peaches
²/₃ cup plus 1 tablespoon sugar
¹/₄ cup tapioca
3 tablespoons flour
1 tablespoon lemon juice

1. Preheat oven to 375°F.

2. Roll out half of pastry dough and place in a 9-inch pie pan.

3. Mix peaches, ²/₃ cup sugar, tapioca, flour and lemon juice in a large bowl. Pour into the pastry-lined pie shell.

4. Roll out remaining dough and place over the filling. Seal the edges. Cut slits in the top. Sprinkle lightly with remaining 1 tablespoon sugar.

5. Place foil over the top and bake for 25 minutes. Remove foil and bake for another 35 minutes, or until the juices bubble and the crust is a deep golden brown. Makes 8 servings.

Asian Pear Tart
KINGSBURG ORCHARDS ◀

CRUST

1 ¹/₃ cups flour
¹/₃ cup packed dark brown sugar
¹/₃ cup finely chopped pecans
¹/₂ teaspoon ground cinnamon
¹/₈ teaspoon salt
²/₃ cup butter, softened

FILLING

3 Kingsburg Orchards* Asian pears (about 2 pounds)
¹/₃ cup butter
¹/₃ cup packed dark brown sugar
1 ¹/₂ teaspoons ground cinnamon
¹/₃ cup toasted chopped pecans

1. Preheat oven to 375°F.
2. To prepare the crust, mix the first 5 ingredients in a medium bowl; cut in the softened butter until crumbly.
3. Press dough firmly and evenly against the bottom and sides of an ungreased 10-inch fluted tart pan.
4. Bake for 15-20 minutes, or until crust is golden brown. Set aside.
5. To prepare the filling, cut Asian pears in half and core, then cut each half into 6 wedges.
6. Melt butter in a large skillet over medium heat; add pears and sauté for 20-25 minutes, or until nearly tender. Add brown sugar and cinnamon; sauté for another 5 minutes or so, until pears are tender.
7. Place sautéed pears in a pinwheel pattern on the crust, and pour remaining sauce from the pan over them. Sprinkle with toasted pecans.
8. Serve with ice cream. Makes 8 servings.

* Brands may vary by region; substitute a similar product.

Watermelon Ice Cream Pie
DULCINEA ▲

24 graham cracker squares
¹/₄ cup corn oil margarine, melted
1 cup chopped Dulcinea* PureHeart Seedless Watermelon
1 quart vanilla ice cream, softened

1. Place 4 graham cracker squares in a blender and process on low speed for 10-15 seconds, or until fine crumbs form. Empty into a medium bowl. Repeat with remaining crackers.
2. Add melted margarine to the cracker crumbs and mix until a ball forms. Press mixture into a 9-inch pie pan. Refrigerate for 1 hour.
3. Place watermelon in a blender, cover and blend on low speed for 30 seconds, or until pureed.
4. Swirl watermelon through softened ice cream.
5. Firmly pack ice cream into the crust. Cover and freeze for several hours, or until firm. Garnish with watermelon balls if desired. Makes 6-8 servings.

* Brands may vary by region; substitute a similar product.

Desperts ▌

Lemon Cake
BEE SWEET CITRUS

1 ³/₄ cups sugar, divided
1 cup butter, softened
2 large eggs
2 teaspoons vanilla extract
2 ¹/₂ cups flour
1 teaspoon baking powder
¹/₂ teaspoon salt
1 teaspoon baking soda
1 cup buttermilk
Grated peel and juice of 3 Bee
   Sweet lemons
2 tablespoons poppy seeds

1. Preheat oven to 350°F.
2. In a mixing bowl, cream 1 cup sugar and butter. Blend in eggs and vanilla.
3. In a separate bowl, combine flour, baking powder and salt. Stir into the batter.
4. Stir baking soda into buttermilk and add to the batter.
5. Fold in grated lemon peel and poppy seeds.
6. Pour batter into a greased bundt pan. Bake for 40-50 minutes, or until the cake is golden brown and has a crevice in the middle.
7. Meanwhile, combine lemon juice (about 1 cup) and ³/₄ cup sugar in a saucepan and simmer over low heat until the sugar dissolves.
8. When the cake is done, let stand for 5 minutes, then drizzle sweetened lemon juice slowly over the top until it is all absorbed. Makes 10 servings.

Cocoa Pudding Cake
CONAGRA

1 cup all-purpose flour
¹/₂ cup sugar
¹/₄ cup unsweetened cocoa
1 ¹/₂ teaspoons baking powder
¹/₄ teaspoon salt
³/₄ cup milk
2 tablespoons margarine, melted
1 teaspoon vanilla extract
3 1-ounce envelopes Swiss Miss* Milk Chocolate Hot Cocoa Mix
1 ¹/₂ cups boiling water
Reddi-wip* Original or Chocolate Whipped Light Cream

1. Preheat oven to 350°F.
2. Combine flour, sugar, cocoa, baking powder and salt in a large mixing bowl. Add milk, margarine and vanilla; mix until blended and smooth.
3. Spoon batter into an ungreased 9-by-9-inch baking pan.
4. Place cocoa mix in a medium bowl. Add boiling water and mix well. Pour evenly over the batter.
5. Bake for 30 minutes, or until the top is firm to the touch.
6. Let the cake cool for 10 minutes. Serve warm with Reddi-wip. Makes 8 servings.

Brands may vary by region; substitute a similar product.

ConAgra Foods®

Whipped Vanilla Cream with Arils
POM WONDERFUL ▼

1 large fresh Pom Wonderful pomegranate
1 cup very cold heavy cream
2 tablespoons confectioners' sugar
2 teaspoons vanilla extract

1. Score pomegranate and place in a bowl of water. Break open the pomegranate underwater to free the arils (seed sacs). The arils will sink to the bottom of the bowl and the membrane will float to the top. Drain the arils in a sieve and place in a separate bowl. Reserve ¼ cup of the arils and set aside. (Refrigerate or freeze remaining arils for another use, or serve separately.)

2. In a medium bowl, beat cream with a wire whisk or electric mixer until slightly thickened.

3. Add confectioners' sugar and vanilla, and whip until the mixture doubles in volume and soft peaks form. Gently fold in ¼ cup arils.

4. Serve the cream mixture immediately over your favorite cake or pie. Makes 4-6 servings.

Variations: Add ¼ teaspoon ground cinnamon, ¼ teaspoon ground ginger or ¼ teaspoon espresso powder along with vanilla.

Gingerbread Cake
SPLENDA ▲

Butter-flavored cooking spray
2 cups unsweetened applesauce
3/4 cup molasses
1/3 cup vegetable oil
3 large eggs
3 cups all-purpose flour
1 1/3 cups Splenda No Calorie
    Sweetener, Granular
2 teaspoons baking soda
1 teaspoon baking powder
1/2 teaspoon salt
2 teaspoons ground ginger
1 1/2 teaspoons ground cinnamon
1/2 teaspoon ground cloves

1. Preheat oven to 350°F. Coat a 10-cup bundt pan with cooking spray.
Set aside.

2. Pour applesauce, molasses and vegetable oil into a large mixing bowl.
Add eggs and stir well.

3. Blend remaining ingredients in a separate bowl. Add to the applesauce
mixture and stir until well blended.

4. Pour cake batter into the prepared pan. Bake for 50-60 minutes, or until
a toothpick inserted in the center comes out clean.

5. Cool cake in the pan on a wire rack. Invert cake onto a serving plate.
Makes 18 servings.

Serving suggestion: Top with raspberries or other fresh fruit.

Best Ever Banana Angel Cake
BONITA BANANA ▲

1 1/2 cups flour
1/2 teaspoon baking powder
1/2 teaspoon baking soda
7 large eggs, separated
1/2 teaspoon cream of tartar
2 ripe Bonita* bananas
1 1/2 cups granulated sugar
1/2 cup vegetable oil

TOPPING
1/2 stick butter
1/2 cup brown sugar
1/4 cup milk
1 cup confectioners' sugar
2 ripe Bonita* bananas, peeled
    and sliced

1. Preheat oven to 325°F.

2. Sift flour, baking powder and baking soda into a bowl.

3. Beat egg whites in another bowl. Add cream of tartar and continue
beating until fluffy.

4. Mash 2 bananas in a large bowl. Add egg yolks, sugar and oil, and beat
until creamy.

5. Stir in sifted flour. Fold in egg whites.

6. Pour into a greased angel food cake pan and bake for 55 minutes.
Let cool in pan.

7. To prepare the topping, place butter and brown sugar in a saucepan
and melt over medium heat. Stir in milk and confectioners' sugar.

8. Decorate cake with sliced bananas and caramel sauce. Makes 8 servings.

* Brands may vary by region; substitute a similar product.

Holiday Mini Cakes
JELLY BELLY ▼

1 10 ¾-ounce package frozen pound cake, thawed
2 cups confectioners' sugar
3-4 tablespoons milk
Food coloring
Flavored extract, to taste
5 ounces Jelly Belly jelly beans

1. Trim dark crust from top and sides of cake. Cut cake in half horizontally.
2. Using a 3 ½-inch cookie cutter (egg or bunny for Easter; tree or wreath for Christmas; hearts for Valentine's Day; flowers for Mother's Day), cut 3 mini cakes from each half of the pound cake.

3. Place mini cakes on a wire rack over a large bowl; set aside.
4. In another bowl, stir confectioners' sugar and milk until smooth. Tint with food coloring and flavor with extract if desired.
5. Spoon icing over mini cakes, allowing excess to drip into bowl.
6. When icing bowl is empty, place rack of mini cakes over empty icing bowl.
7. Decorate mini cakes with jelly beans. Refrigerate until icing is set, about 20 minutes.
8. Wrap in plastic wrap until ready to serve. Makes 6 servings.

Triple Chocolate Brownies with Cookie Bottoms
BARRY CALLEBAUT

7 ¹/₂ ounces flour
2 ounces Dutch cocoa powder
¹/₄ teaspoon baking powder
¹/₄ teaspoon salt
6 ¹/₄ ounces bittersweet chocolate
8 ounces butter
1 ¹/₂ teaspoons vanilla extract
5 large eggs
15 ounces granulated sugar
4 ounces Belgian chocolate chunks
8 Kirkland Signature chocolate chunk cookies, crushed

1. Preheat oven to 325°F.
2. In a bowl, mix together flour, cocoa, baking powder and salt.
3. Melt bittersweet chocolate and butter. Stir in vanilla. Let cool slightly.
4. In a separate bowl, mix together eggs and sugar. Add chocolate mixture and stir to blend.
5. Fold in flour mixture and half of the chocolate chunks.
6. Place crushed cookies in a greased 13-by-9- or 12-by-8-inch baking pan.
7. Place brownie mixture on top of crushed cookies.
8. Top with remaining chocolate chunks.
9. Bake for 30-35 minutes, or until a toothpick inserted in the center comes out clean. Makes 12 brownies.

Famous Fudge
NESTLÉ TOLL HOUSE

1 ¹/₂ cups granulated sugar
²/₃ cup (5-ounce can) Nestlé Carnation Evaporated Milk
2 tablespoons butter or margarine
¹/₄ teaspoon salt
2 cups miniature marshmallows
1 ¹/₂ cups (9 ounces) Nestlé Toll House Semi-Sweet Chocolate Morsels
¹/₂ cup chopped pecans or walnuts (optional)
1 teaspoon vanilla extract

1. Line an 8-inch square baking pan with foil.
2. Combine sugar, evaporated milk, butter and salt in a medium heavy-duty saucepan. Bring to a full rolling boil over medium heat, stirring constantly. Boil, stirring constantly, for 4-5 minutes. Remove from heat.
3. Stir in marshmallows, morsels, nuts and vanilla extract. Stir vigorously for 1 minute, or until marshmallows are melted.
4. Pour into prepared baking pan. Refrigerate for 2 hours, or until firm.
5. Lift fudge from the pan and remove foil. Cut into pieces. Makes 49 pieces.

Colorful Cheesecake Bars
M&M'S

2 lemons
1/4 pound unsalted butter, softened
1 cup sugar, divided
1/2 teaspoon salt
1 1/4 cups flour
16 ounces cream cheese, softened
3 large eggs
1 cup M&M'S Chocolate Candies

1. Line a 9-inch square baking pan with foil.

2. Squeeze lemons; you should get about 4-6 tablespoons of juice.

3. Place butter, 1/4 cup sugar and salt in a mixing bowl and beat until smooth. Fold in flour. Add 2 tablespoons lemon juice. Press mixture into the pan; refrigerate for 30 minutes.

4. Preheat oven to 350°F.

5. Remove crust from the fridge and bake for 20 minutes.

6. Place cream cheese and remaining 3/4 cup sugar in a mixing bowl and beat until smooth. Beat in eggs one at a time. Add 2 tablespoons lemon juice.

7. Pour cream cheese mixture over the crust.

8. Bake for 40 minutes, or until set. Remove from the oven and let cool to room temperature.

9. Top with M&M'S and refrigerate overnight. Cut into triangle shapes. Makes about 32 bars.

Berry Cherry Oatmeal Cookie Bars
MEDURI FARMS

2 cups all-purpose flour
1 teaspoon baking soda
1/2 teaspoon salt
1 teaspoon ground cinnamon
1 cup butter, softened
3/4 cup granulated sugar
3/4 cup firmly packed
   brown sugar
1 teaspoon pure vanilla extract
2 large eggs
2 1/4 cups quick oats, uncooked
1 cup Meduri Farms* dried
   blueberries
1 cup Meduri Farms* dried
   tart cherries
1/2 cup chopped walnuts

1. Preheat oven to 375°F.

2. In a small bowl, combine flour, baking soda, salt and cinnamon; set aside.

3. In a large bowl, beat butter, granulated sugar, brown sugar and vanilla extract until creamy. Beat in eggs.

4. Gradually beat in flour mixture. Stir in oats, dried blueberries, dried cherries and walnuts.

5. Spread dough into an ungreased 13-by-9-inch baking pan. Bake for 22-25 minutes, or until bars are light brown and a toothpick inserted in the center comes out clean.

6. Cool completely in the pan on a wire rack. Cut into 24 squares.

7. Top with ice cream for dessert or enjoy for breakfast. Makes 24 servings.

Brands may vary by region; substitute a similar product.

Cashew Oatmeal Bars
HARVEST MANOR FARMS ▲

³/₄ cup whole wheat flour

³/₄ cup unbleached all-purpose flour

1 teaspoon ground cinnamon

¹/₂ teaspoon kosher salt

1 stick (4 ounces) unsalted butter, at room temperature

¹/₂ cup honey

¹/₃ cup packed brown sugar

2 large eggs

³/₄ cup old-fashioned oats

¹/₂ cup sweetened dried cranberries

4 ounces bittersweet chocolate, chopped*

1 cup Kirkland Signature roasted and salted cashews, coarsely chopped

1. Preheat oven to 350°F. Butter and flour a 13-by-9-inch baking pan.

2. In a bowl, sift together flours, cinnamon and salt; set aside.

3. With an electric mixer, cream butter, honey and sugar until light and fluffy. Beat in eggs one at a time until fully incorporated and mixture is smooth.

4. Add sifted ingredients and mix until just blended.

5. Fold in oats, cranberries, chocolate and cashews. Mixture will be very stiff.

6. Using a wooden spatula, spread mixture evenly in the prepared pan.

7. Bake for 23-30 minutes, or until golden brown.

8. Let cool on a rack for 10 minutes and then cut into squares.

Makes 15-24 servings.

Tip: These are very rich; a little goes a long way.

You can use semisweet chips for a sweeter bar, but the purer the chocolate, the less sugar and the more flavonoids (antioxidants) it has.

Cashew Brittle
ANN'S HOUSE OF NUTS ▲

1 cup sugar

¹/₂ cup light corn syrup

1 ¹/₂ cups Kirkland Signature roasted and salted cashews (halves)

1 teaspoon butter

1 teaspoon baking soda

1 teaspoon vanilla extract

1. Combine sugar and corn syrup in a microwave-safe bowl. Microwave, uncovered, for 4 minutes on high; stir, then heat for 3 minutes longer.

2. Stir in cashews and butter. Microwave for 30-60 seconds on high, or until the mixture turns light amber (mixture will be very hot).

3. Quickly stir in baking soda and vanilla until light and foamy.

4. Immediately pour onto a greased baking sheet and spread with a metal spatula.

5. Refrigerate for 20 minutes, or until set.

6. Break into small pieces. Store in an airtight container. Makes 16 servings.

❙ Desserts

Poppy's Cookies

1 1/2 cups butter, softened

12 ounces cream cheese, softened

4 1/2 cups all-purpose flour

16 ounces (1 pound) Walls Berry Farm* ⓤOrganic
Organic Strawberry Preserves

1. Place butter and cream cheese in a bowl and beat with an electric mixer until softened and thoroughly blended.

2. Slowly mix in flour, beating until thoroughly blended.

3. Roll dough into 1-inch balls. Cover with plastic wrap and refrigerate for at least 8 hours.

4. Preheat oven to 350°F.

5. Roll or press dough balls flat. Place 1/2 teaspoon strawberry preserves in the center of each cookie. Fold sides upward and pinch closed. Place on an ungreased cookie sheet.

6. Bake for 20-25 minutes, or until golden brown. Cool on the pan for 5 minutes. Makes 26-30 cookies.

Brands may vary by region; substitute a similar product.

Chunky Banana Nut Cookie
J&J SNACK FOODS ▲

2 Kirkland Signature oatmeal raisin cookies

1/2 cup marshmallow fluff and/or chocolate-hazelnut spread

1/2 banana, diced in 1/4-inch pieces

1/2 cup of your favorite chopped nuts

1. Place 1 cookie flat side up on a dessert plate.

2. Spread half of the marshmallow fluff and/or chocolate-hazelnut spread on the cookie.

3. Top with diced banana and sprinkle with chopped nuts.

4. Spread remaining marshmallow fluff and/or chocolate-hazelnut spread on the second cookie and place on top. Makes 1 serving.

Original Chocolate Chip Cookies
NESTLÉ TOLL HOUSE ▲

2 ¼ cups all-purpose flour

1 teaspoon baking soda

1 teaspoon salt

1 cup (2 sticks) butter, softened

¾ cup granulated sugar

¾ cup packed brown sugar

1 teaspoon vanilla extract

2 large eggs

2 cups Nestlé Toll House Semi-Sweet Chocolate Morsels

1 cup chopped nuts

1. Preheat oven to 375°F.

2. Combine flour, baking soda and salt in a small bowl.

3. Place butter, granulated sugar, brown sugar and vanilla extract in a large mixer bowl and beat until creamy.

4. Add eggs one at a time, beating well after each addition.

5. Gradually beat in flour mixture.

6. Stir in morsels and nuts.

7. Drop by rounded tablespoonfuls onto ungreased baking sheets.

8. Bake for 9-11 minutes, or until golden brown. Cool on baking sheets for 2 minutes; remove to wire racks to cool completely. Makes about 5 dozen cookies.

Pan cookie variation: Grease a 15-by-10-inch jelly-roll pan. Spread dough into the pan. Bake for 20-25 minutes, or until golden brown. Cool in the pan on a wire rack. Makes 4 dozen bars.

Sugared Ginger Cookies
CREATE A TREAT ▲

A classic part of any traditional winter display is a gingerbread house. Thanks to Create A Treat, you can get a premade, ready-to-assemble Gingerbread House Kit. The kit includes the gingerbread forms, candy and premade icing necessary to build your own gingerbread house. Create precious memories while assembling the house—and bake a batch of these Sugared Ginger Cookies to enjoy at the same time.

1 cup unsalted butter, softened

1 cup packed dark brown sugar

½ cup granulated sugar, plus more for coating

1 large egg

½ cup dark molasses

1 teaspoon baking soda

½ teaspoon salt

1 tablespoon ground ginger

½ teaspoon ground cloves

3 ½-4 cups flour

1. Preheat oven to 350°F.

2. Cream butter, brown sugar and ½ cup granulated sugar until light and fluffy. Add egg and molasses; beat until well blended. Add dry ingredients and mix well.

3. Shape the dough into 1-inch balls. Roll in sugar to coat and place on a lightly greased cookie sheet.

4. Bake for 12-15 minutes. Remove from the pan and cool on a wire rack. Makes 3 dozen cookies.

Variation: Form cookie dough into 2-inch-diameter logs and slice in ¼-inch rounds. Either sprinkle with sugar before baking or decorate after baking with icing and candies.

Recipe created by Linda Carey, culinary specialist.

Rugala with Crème Anglaise
COUNTRYSIDE BAKING ▲

1 cup heavy cream
2 teaspoons vanilla extract
4 egg yolks
¹/₃ cup sugar
8 pieces Countryside* Raspberry Rugala
4 teaspoons prepared raspberry sauce or melted raspberry jam
4 tablespoons diced walnuts

1. In a small heavy saucepan, combine cream and vanilla; warm over medium heat until bubbles form.
2. While cream is heating, place egg yolks and sugar in a bowl and whisk until smooth.
3. Remove ¹/₂ cup of heated cream from the saucepan and slowly whisk into the egg mixture.
4. Once combined, gradually whisk mixture back into remaining cream in the saucepan. Cook over medium-low heat, stirring constantly, until the mixture coats the back of a spoon.
5. To serve, spoon a thick layer of crème anglaise onto 4 small plates. Place rugala pieces on crème anglaise. Drizzle with raspberry sauce and top with diced walnuts. Makes 4 servings.

Brands may vary by region; substitute a similar product.

Blueberry-Lemon Squares
GROWER DIRECT/WESTERN SWEET CHERRY ▲

CRUST
¹/₂ cup all-purpose flour
³/₄ cup yellow cornmeal
7 tablespoons confectioners' sugar
¹/₂ teaspoon salt
1 stick (¹/₂ cup) cold unsalted butter, cut into pieces

FILLING
3 large eggs
¹/₂ cup granulated sugar

1 ¹/₂ tablespoons all-purpose flour
1 ¹/₂ teaspoons finely grated fresh lemon peel
2 tablespoons fresh lemon juice
2 tablespoons light cream
Salt
2 cups (10 ounces) Grower Direct* blueberries
4 tablespoons blueberry jam, melted and strained

1. Preheat oven to 375°F. Line a buttered 8-inch square glass pan with two 18-by-6-inch sheets of foil, overlapping in opposite directions with overhang on all sides.
2. To prepare the crust, place all ingredients in a food processor and pulse until mixture resembles coarse meal. Press onto the bottom and 1 inch up the sides of the pan. Bake on the middle oven rack for 20 minutes, or until golden brown.
3. To prepare the filling, whisk together eggs, sugar, flour and grated peel. Whisk in lemon juice, cream and a pinch of salt. Pour immediately into the hot crust. Bake until just set, about 17 minutes.
4. Toss blueberries with jam; gently spoon over the top and bake 2 minutes longer. Let cool in the pan on a rack. Chill, covered, overnight (8 hours). Lift dessert out of the pan and cut into squares. Makes 12 servings.

Brands may vary by region; substitute a similar product.

Butter Croissant Pudding
VIE DE FRANCE ◀

6 large Vie de France butter croissants
3 large eggs
1 1/4 cups milk
1 1/4 cups heavy cream
1/2 cup sugar
1/2 teaspoon vanilla extract
Butter
1/4 cup dark raisins
3 tablespoons apricot jam
Confectioners' sugar

1. Preheat oven to 325°F.
2. Cut croissants into pieces.
3. Combine eggs, milk and cream in a large bowl. Add sugar and vanilla. Mix until well blended.
4. Generously butter a 2 1/2-quart baking dish. Layer the croissant pieces in the dish. Sprinkle raisins over each layer.
5. Pour egg mixture over the croissants and let stand for 15 minutes, pressing down on the croissants with a wooden spoon to soak completely.
6. Place the baking dish in a large roasting pan and fill the pan with hot water halfway up the sides of the dish.
7. Bake for 40-45 minutes, or until firm and golden brown. Remove from the oven and let cool.
8. Heat jam until melted, brush over the baked pudding and let cool completely. Sprinkle with confectioners' sugar. Makes 10-12 servings.
Tip: Butter Croissant Pudding can be stored, covered, in the refrigerator for up to 2 days.

Sugar and Spice Muffins
KRUSTEAZ ▲

2 1/2 cups Krusteaz Buttermilk Pancake Mix
2/3 cup water
1/2 cup sugar
1/4 cup vegetable oil
1 large egg
1/2 teaspoon grated nutmeg

TOPPING
4 tablespoons butter
1/2 cup sugar
2 teaspoons ground cinnamon

1. Preheat oven to 400°F.
2. In a medium bowl, stir together pancake mix, water, sugar, vegetable oil, egg and nutmeg until just blended.
3. Spoon batter into a lightly greased or paper-lined 12-cup muffin pan, filling two-thirds full.
4. Bake for 12-14 minutes, or until a toothpick inserted in the center comes out clean.
5. To prepare the topping, melt butter and set aside. In a small bowl, stir together sugar and cinnamon.
6. While muffins are still warm from the oven, dip into melted butter and then cinnamon-sugar mixture. Makes 12 servings.

KRUSTEAZ

Desserts ▌

Washington Apple Bread with Streusel Topping
HOLTZINGER FRUIT ▼

APPLE BREAD
2 cups flour
1 teaspoon baking soda
1/4 teaspoon salt
1/2 cup (1 stick) butter, softened
1 cup sugar
2 large eggs
1 tablespoon lemon juice
2 teaspoons vanilla extract

2 Holtzinger Fruit Granny Smith apples (or apple of choice), peeled and chopped

STREUSEL TOPPING
2 tablespoons flour
2 tablespoons granulated sugar
1 teaspoon ground cinnamon
1 tablespoon butter
2 tablespoons brown sugar

1. Preheat oven to 350°F.

2. To prepare the topping, combine flour, granulated sugar and cinnamon in a small bowl. Cut in butter until crumbly. Set aside.

3. To prepare the bread, combine flour, baking soda and salt in a medium bowl.

4. Cream butter and sugar in a mixing bowl. Beat in eggs, lemon juice and vanilla.

5. Add the flour mixture to the butter mixture and stir just until moistened. Add apples and stir gently to combine.

6. Spoon half of the batter into a buttered 9-by-5-inch loaf pan. Sprinkle with half of the topping. Spoon remaining batter into the pan and sprinkle with the remaining topping. Finish by sprinkling evenly with brown sugar.

7. Bake for 55-60 minutes, or until a wooden pick inserted in the center comes out clean. Remove the bread from the pan and set on a rack to cool. Makes 10 servings.

Coffee Danish Explosion
KIRKLAND SIGNATURE/PURATOS ▼

¹/₂ cup butter, softened
1 cup packed light brown sugar
8 assorted Kirkland Signature Danish pastries
4 cups granola, plus more for garnish
Whipped topping
Instant espresso powder
Melted chocolate or chocolate syrup

CUSTARD
3 large eggs
2 cups heavy cream
1 can sweetened condensed milk
2 tablespoons vanilla extract (preferably Bourbon vanilla)

1. Preheat oven to 350°F.

2. Grease 8 cups of a deep muffin pan with butter. Add brown sugar to the bottom of each cup and press firmly.

3. Place 1 Danish in each muffin cup, leaving the center hollow.

4. To prepare the custard, place eggs in a mixing bowl and beat for 1 minute. Add cream, condensed milk and vanilla, stirring to blend well.

5. Pour custard into the center of each Danish. Top with granola.

6. Bake for 30 minutes, or until custard is set. Let cool for 30 minutes on a rack.

7. Flavor your favorite whipped topping with espresso powder.

8. To serve, garnish with whipped topping, chocolate and granola.

Makes 8 servings.

Puratos
Reliable partners in innovation

Desserts |

Churros Spanish-Style (Churros con Chocolate)
J&J SNACK FOODS ▼

Take home some delicious Double Twisted Churros from Costco's Food Court, or prepare J&J Snack Foods' Gourmet Double Twisted Churros (available in Costco's freezer case), following the directions on the package.

While the churros are warming, prepare this delicious authentic chocolate dip to dunk them in.

CHOCOLATE DIP
4 ounces dark chocolate
2 cups milk, divided
1 tablespoon cornstarch
4 tablespoons sugar

1. Place chocolate and 1 cup milk in a saucepan over medium heat. Stir until chocolate melts.
2. Dissolve cornstarch in the remaining milk. Using a whisk, slowly add to the melted chocolate mixture.
3. Whisk in sugar.
4. Reduce heat to low and cook, whisking constantly, until it thickens, about 5 minutes.
5. Remove from the heat and continue to whisk until smooth.
6. Serve the warm chocolate dip in a coffee cup. Dunk the churros into the chocolate dip to enjoy as the Spanish do! Makes 2 servings.

Apple Cheddar Pizza with Toasted Pecans
L&M ▼

Vegetable oil cooking spray
1 12-ounce can refrigerated pizza crust dough
3 large L&M* Fuji or Granny Smith apples, peeled, cored and thinly sliced
1 cup apple juice
1 tablespoon cornstarch
1/2 teaspoon ground cinnamon
2 tablespoons honey
1/4 cup chopped toasted pecans
1 cup grated white Cheddar cheese

1. Preheat oven to 425°F.
2. Lightly coat a 14-inch pizza pan with cooking spray. Press dough into the pan.
3. Place apples and apple juice in a saucepan and simmer until tender. Drain off juice and reserve. Spread apple slices over the dough.
4. Return reserved apple juice to the saucepan and stir in cornstarch, cinnamon and honey. Cook over medium heat until clear. Spread sauce over apples.
5. Sprinkle pecans over apples. Top with cheese.
6. Bake for 15-20 minutes, or until the crust is golden brown. Makes 8 servings.

Brands may vary by region; substitute a similar product.

Vanilla Ice Cream Waffles
KIRKLAND SIGNATURE ◄

2 1/2 cups Kirkland Signature vanilla ice cream, plus more for topping
2 large eggs
1/4 teaspoon salt
2 cups all-purpose flour
Cooking oil or spray
1 cup fresh sliced strawberries, raspberries, blackberries or blueberries

1. Preheat a waffle iron according to manufacturer's instructions. Preheat oven to 200°F.

2. Place 2 1/2 cups ice cream in a bowl. Melt in a microwave using the defrost cycle. Ice cream must be thoroughly melted.

3. In a separate bowl, beat eggs with a whisk until they are pale yellow. Add eggs to the melted ice cream and whisk to blend.

4. Whisk in salt and flour until just combined.

5. Lightly coat the waffle iron with cooking oil using a pastry brush or with cooking spray.

6. For each waffle, measure about 1/2 cup of batter and pour over the waffle-iron grid to cover. Cook for 4-6 minutes, or until golden brown.

7. Transfer waffles to a baking sheet and keep warm in the oven until ready to serve.

8. Top waffles with ice cream and berries. Makes 4 servings (8 waffles).

Cherry Berry Crisps
QUAKER ▲

1/2 cup granulated sugar
1 tablespoon cornstarch
1/2 cup cranberry juice or Tropicana orange juice
2 16-ounce cans pitted sour cherries, drained
1/3 cup sweetened dried cranberries
3/4 cup Quaker Oats (quick or old-fashioned, uncooked)
3 tablespoons firmly packed brown sugar
2 tablespoons margarine or butter, melted
1 tablespoon all-purpose flour
1/4 teaspoon ground cinnamon

1. Preheat oven to 375°F.

2. In a medium saucepan, stir together granulated sugar and cornstarch. Gradually stir in cranberry juice, mixing well. Stirring constantly, bring to a boil over medium-high heat. Cook and stir for 1 minute, or until thickened and clear.

3. Remove from the heat and stir in cherries and cranberries.

4. Spoon filling into 6 small (about 6-ounce) ovenproof custard or soufflé cups or ramekins, dividing evenly.

5. Combine oats, brown sugar, margarine, flour and cinnamon in a small bowl and mix well. Sprinkle evenly over fruit cups.

6. Bake for 15-20 minutes, or until the topping is golden brown. Serve warm. Makes 6 servings.

Tropicana

Mango Cobbler
FRESKA PRODUCE ▲

4 Freska* ripe mangoes, peeled and sliced
1 teaspoon ground ginger
1 teaspoon ground cinnamon
$1/2$ cup fresh orange juice

TOPPING
1 cup unbleached flour
1 tablespoon sugar
$1/4$ teaspoon fine sea salt
1 $1/2$ teaspoons baking powder
3 tablespoons unsalted butter, at room temperature
1 $1/2$ cups milk
$1/4$ cup confectioners' sugar

1. Preheat oven to 350°F.
2. In a 9-inch square baking dish, combine mangoes, ginger, cinnamon and orange juice. Toss together to coat.
3. To prepare the topping, combine flour, sugar, salt and baking powder in a small bowl; stir to blend. Add butter and mix until it has a sandy consistency. Stir in milk until smooth.
4. Dollop the topping onto the mango mixture, spreading to cover most of the surface.
5. Bake for 25 minutes, or until golden brown. Dust with confectioners' sugar and serve warm. Makes 6 servings.

Recipe provided by Chef Allen Susser, The Great Mango Book (Ten Speed Press, 2001).
* Brands may vary by region; substitute a similar product.

100% Fruit Juice Gelatin Cutouts
APPLE & EVE ▲

4 1-ounce envelopes Knox Unflavored Gelatine
5 6 $3/4$-ounce boxes Apple & Eve* 100% Apple Juice
2 15-ounce cans mandarin oranges, drained
2 tablespoons honey or sugar

1. In a large bowl, mix gelatin with contents of 1 juice box.
2. Pour contents of remaining 4 juice boxes into a saucepan and bring to a boil. Add hot juice to the gelatin mixture and stir until all ingredients are dissolved. Refrigerate until gelatin is slightly thickened.
3. Stir in mandarin oranges and honey.
4. Pour into a 13-by-9-inch pan and chill until firm.
5. Cut into fun shapes with a variety of cookie cutters. Makes 6-10 servings.

* Brands may vary by region; substitute a similar product.

Orange Mango Pudding
READY PAC ▼

1 1/2 cups orange segments, plus more for garnish
2 cups Ready Pac* fresh-cut mangoes cut in 1/2-inch cubes
1 cup fresh orange juice
2 tablespoons fresh lemon juice
1/2 cup milk
1/2 cup heavy cream
1 package unflavored gelatin
1 cup sugar

1. In a blender, combine 1 1/2 cups orange segments, mango, orange juice and lemon juice, and puree until smooth.

2. In a medium saucepan, combine milk, cream, gelatin and sugar. Bring to a simmer over medium-low heat, stirring to dissolve the gelatin and melt the sugar, 2-3 minutes.

3. Remove the saucepan from the heat. Pour the pureed mango mixture into the saucepan and mix well (if a very smooth consistency is desired, strain the mango mixture into the saucepan).

4. Pour the mixture into a 1-quart mold or divide among 4 individual 1-cup ramekins.

5. Cover and refrigerate until firm, 3-4 hours, or overnight.

6. To serve, garnish with orange segments. Makes 4 servings.

* Brands may vary by region; substitute a similar product.

Desserts

Ambrosia Salad
DANNON

1 cup miniature marshmallows

1 20-ounce can pineapple chunks, well drained, or 2 cups fresh

1 banana, peeled and sliced

1 11-ounce can mandarin orange segments, well drained

3/4 cup Dannon* Light 'n Fit strawberry nonfat yogurt

1/4 cup toasted coconut flakes

1. Mix all ingredients except coconut in a bowl.

2. Refrigerate for at least 15 minutes.

3. Stir in coconut just before serving. Makes 6-8 servings.

* Brands may vary by region; substitute a similar product.

Grilled Peaches
SunWest

Oil or cooking spray

8 firm SunWest California peaches

48 whole cloves

1 cup sugar

1 teaspoon ground cinnamon

Heavy-duty aluminum foil

Mint sprigs, for garnish

1. Preheat a gas or charcoal grill. Lightly spray grill with oil or cooking spray.

2. Bring a large pot of water to a boil. Carve an X on the bottom of each peach. Immerse peaches in boiling water for 30 seconds. Remove and immediately plunge into ice water. When cool, gently pull off the skin with a paring knife.

3. Stick 6 cloves into each peach.

4. In a small bowl, combine sugar and cinnamon. Roll peaches in the mixture.

5. Place each peach, stem side down, on a square of aluminum foil. Sprinkle remaining cinnamon sugar over peaches and tightly close foil around each peach.

6. Place packets on gas grill over low heat or charcoal grill 5-6 inches from coals. Cook for 10 minutes, or until heated through.

7. Carefully open each packet in a serving bowl to capture all the juice. Discard the cloves. Garnish with mint sprigs and serve hot or cold with ice cream for dessert or as a side dish. Makes 8 servings.

Tip: Grilled peaches freeze well or can be refrigerated for a week.

Peach Panini
TRINITY FRUIT ▼

1 16-ounce Sara Lee pound cake, thawed
1 stick ($^1/_2$ cup) salted butter, softened
1 $^1/_4$ cups packed dark brown sugar
10 Trinity Fruit white flesh peaches
$^1/_2$ cup plus $^1/_3$ cup granulated sugar
1 12-ounce package frozen raspberries, thawed
1 pint heavy whipping cream
$^1/_4$ cup Torani vanilla syrup
Fresh raspberries and mint sprigs, for garnish

1. Cut cake into ten $^3/_4$-inch slices. Butter both sides of each slice. Spread 1 tablespoon brown sugar on each side of cake slices.

2. Place cake slices in a preheated panini maker for 40 seconds, or until golden brown. Remove to a sheet of waxed paper to cool. Slice each piece in half diagonally.

3. Peel and slice peaches into a bowl. Stir in $^1/_2$ cup sugar. Refrigerate.

4. Puree thawed raspberries with remaining $^1/_3$ cup sugar and press through a sieve to remove the seeds. Refrigerate.

5. Beat whipping cream with vanilla syrup until stiff peaks form. Refrigerate.

6. Using a squeeze bottle or pastry bag, squeeze some raspberry sauce onto a serving plate in a zigzag pattern.

7. Place half of the cake slices on top of the sauce, then add the peaches. Stand the remaining cake slices on top of the peaches.

8. Drizzle with remaining raspberry sauce, top with whipped cream and garnish with fresh raspberries and mint. Makes 10 servings.

Recipe created by Trinity's executive chefs: Lisa White, Cindy Parker, Diane Poss and Joanne Weaver.

Sweet Pizza
ACONEX ◄

11 ounces flour

3 tablespoons confectioners' sugar

1/2 teaspoon baking powder

5 1/2 ounces margarine

2 egg yolks

1 teaspoon vanilla extract

1 small box (4-serving size) vanilla pudding mix

2 cups milk

11 ounces seasonal fruit: grapes, plums, kiwis, cherries, seeded or peeled as appropriate

1/4 cup fruit jelly, melted

1 cup sweetened whipped cream

1. Preheat oven to 350°F.

2. In a bowl, sift together flour, sugar and baking powder. Add margarine and blend into the flour mixture. Stir in egg yolks and vanilla. Let rest for 10 minutes.

3. Roll out dough and place in a 10-inch tart pan.

4. Bake for 25 minutes, or until golden brown.

5. Combine pudding mix with milk and cook until thickened. Pour over the pastry and let cool.

6. Arrange fruit on top. Brush with melted jelly.

7. Garnish with whipped cream. Makes 4-6 servings.

Cherry Danish English Trifle with Buttermilk Pastry Cream
COTTAGE BAKERY ▲

2 Kirkland Signature cherry Danish (or any other flavor Danish in variety pack), torn into bite-size pieces

Whipped cream topping

BUTTERMILK PASTRY CREAM

1/2 cup sugar

6 tablespoons all-purpose flour

1/4 teaspoon salt

2 cups buttermilk

4 large egg yolks

1 vanilla bean, split lengthwise

2 tablespoons freshly grated lemon peel

Juice of 1 lemon

1. Prepare Buttermilk Pastry Cream: Whisk together sugar, flour and salt in a small bowl and set aside.

2. Place buttermilk and egg yolks in a saucepan. Scrape the vanilla seeds into the pan and stir to combine.

3. Gradually whisk in flour mixture over medium heat. Whisk constantly until the mixture begins to thicken, about 4 minutes.

4. Stir in grated lemon peel and juice.

5. Pour pastry cream into a bowl, place in an ice bath and let cool completely, stirring occasionally.

6. For each serving, place a small amount of pastry cream in the bottom of a parfait glass. Top with a layer of Danish pieces. Continue layering until the glass is filled.

7. Garnish with your favorite whipped topping. Makes 4-5 servings.

Granola Strawberry Parfait
NATURE'S PATH ORGANIC FOODS ▲

1 1/2 cups low-fat ricotta
1/4 cup low-fat plain yogurt
4-5 tablespoons strawberry jam (depending on desired sweetness)
1 teaspoon grated orange peel
1-1 1/4 pounds strawberries, trimmed
1 1/2 cups Nature's Path Flax Plus Granola ⊌Organic
Fresh mint leaves, for garnish

1. Puree ricotta, yogurt and jam in a food processor. Stir in grated orange peel.
2. Cut strawberries into thick slices.
3. Spoon 2 tablespoons granola into each of 6 tall parfait glasses. Top with 2 tablespoons of ricotta mixture and a thick layer of strawberry slices. Repeat with a second layer of granola, ricotta and strawberries.
4. Garnish with mint leaves.
5. Serve immediately or refrigerate for up to 6 hours. Makes 6 servings.
Tip: If you don't have parfait glasses, use wine goblets or drinking glasses.

Blueberry Trifle with Granola
TOWNSEND FARMS/CURRY & COMPANY/ SUNNYRIDGE FARM ▲

4 cups fresh blueberries
2 cups Kirkland Signature Granola Snack Mix

LEMON PASTRY CREAM
5 large egg yolks
1/2 cup cornstarch
4 cups heavy cream, divided
1/2 cup fresh lemon juice
1 1/2 cups sugar
1/2 teaspoon vanilla extract

1. To prepare pastry cream, combine egg yolks, cornstarch and 1 cup cream in a bowl. Whisk to blend well. Set aside.
2. Combine 2 cups cream, lemon juice and sugar in a saucepan over medium heat. Whisk to dissolve sugar and bring to a boil. Slowly whisk into egg yolk mixture. Pour into a double boiler over simmering water and cook, whisking constantly, for 10 minutes, or until slightly thickened. Stir in vanilla. Pour into a mixing bowl and refrigerate for 1 1/2 hours.
3. When pastry cream is cool, stir in 1 cup cream and beat with an electric mixer fitted with a wire whip until light and fluffy.
4. To assemble, place 1/2 cup blueberries in a large wine glass. Pour 1/2 cup lemon cream on top. Add 1/2 cup granola, then 1/2 cup lemon cream. Top with 1/2 cup blueberries. Serve chilled. Makes 4 servings.
Recipe created by Jean-Yves Mocquet, Costco Foods Assistant General Merchandising Manager.

Orange-Honey Yogurt Parfait with Granola, Oranges and Strawberries
SUNKIST ▼

ORANGE-HONEY YOGURT

24 ounces low-fat vanilla yogurt

8 ounces peeled Sunkist oranges, segmented and chopped

3 tablespoons grated Sunkist orange peel

3 tablespoons orange blossom honey

3 cups granola

12 ounces peeled Sunkist oranges, segmented

12 ounces Sunkist strawberries, trimmed and quartered

Grated Sunkist orange peel, for garnish

1. Prepare Orange-Honey Yogurt: Combine yogurt, chopped orange, grated peel and honey in a large bowl. Whisk until completely combined.

2. For each parfait, spoon 1/4 cup granola into the bottom of an 8-ounce parfait glass.

3. Spoon 1/4 cup Orange-Honey Yogurt onto the granola. Do not push the yogurt to the sides of the glass, as it will spread naturally.

4. Top yogurt with 1 ounce each of orange segments and strawberries.

5. Dollop about 1 tablespoon yogurt on strawberries.

6. Garnish with grated orange peel. Makes 12 servings.

Sunkist

Lemon and Cream Cheese Parfait with Blueberry-Amaretto Compote
RASKAS ▲

1 1/2 pounds Raskas Brand* cream cheese, softened
16 ounces prepared lemon curd
1/2 cup fresh lemon juice
Finely grated peel of 3 lemons
1 cup heavy whipping cream
1/2 cup amaretto liqueur
1/2 cup packed light brown sugar
3 pints fresh blueberries, rinsed and sorted
3 cups prepared sweetened whipped cream
12 fresh mint sprigs

1. Beat cream cheese until light and smooth. Add lemon curd, lemon juice and grated peel; beat until well blended.

2. In another bowl, beat whipping cream until stiff peaks form. Fold into the cream cheese mixture. Transfer to a pastry bag without a tip. Refrigerate.

3. Combine amaretto and brown sugar in a bowl and stir until sugar has dissolved. Stir in blueberries. Let stand for 1 hour.

4. To assemble parfaits, pipe 1/4 cup lemon cream into each of 12 wine goblets. Spoon 2 tablespoons of blueberries over the lemon cream. Repeat with another layer of lemon cream.

5. Top each parfait with a dollop of sweetened whipped cream. Garnish with a mint sprig. Makes 12 servings.

Brands may vary by region; substitute a similar product.

SCHREIBER™

Kirkland Signature Granola Parfait
BEST BRANDS/MULTIFOODS ▲

1 cup Kirkland Signature Granola Snack Mix
4 ounces vanilla yogurt

1. Place one-third of the granola in a parfait glass. Top with half of the yogurt.

2. Repeat with 1 more layer of each.

3. Top with the remaining granola. Makes 1 serving.

Variation: 1 ounce of fresh fruit may be added to each layer or as a topping.

Best Brands Corp.

Grasshopper Parfaits
KRAFT ▼

1 ¹/₂ cups finely chopped OREO Chocolate Sandwich Cookies

¹/₂ cup finely chopped chocolate-covered mint patties

1 quart (4 cups) cold milk

2 packages (4-serving size each) chocolate-flavor instant pudding and pie filling

2-4 drops green food coloring

2 cups frozen whipped dessert topping, thawed

1. Mix chopped cookies and mint patties in a small bowl; set aside.

2. Pour milk into a medium bowl. Add dry pudding mixes. Beat with a wire whisk for 2 minutes. Let stand for 5 minutes.

3. Meanwhile, stir food coloring into whipped topping until well blended.

4. In 12 parfait or dessert glasses, add these layers: pudding, whipped topping, cookie crumble, pudding, whipped topping and cookie crumble.

5. Refrigerate for at least 30 minutes or until ready to serve. Store leftover parfaits in the refrigerator. Makes 12 servings, about ²/₃ cup each.

Beverages

Organic Iced Mocha Martini
SAN FRANCISCO BAY COFFEE ◀

4 cups double-strength brewed San Francisco Bay* Organic
    100% Organic Rainforest Blend Coffee
4 tablespoons chocolate syrup
Organic milk or cream to taste, if desired
Liqueur of choice (optional)
Cinnamon (optional)

1. For double-strength coffee, use your normal brewing method and either double the amount of coffee or use half as much water.

2. For each serving, measure out 1 cup of coffee. Add 1 tablespoon chocolate syrup (or more to taste) and stir to dissolve. Stir in milk or cream, if desired.

3. Fill a martini/cocktail shaker three-quarters full of ice.

4. Pour sweetened coffee into the shaker. Add liqueur, if desired.

5. Shake, shake, shake until the shaker is frosty or your hand gets a bit cold.

6. Strain iced coffee into a martini glass and sprinkle with cinnamon, if desired.

7. Repeat for remaining 3 servings. Makes 4 servings.

Tip: We think the best-tasting iced coffee is made with fresh-brewed coffee chilled in an ice-filled martini shaker, which locks in flavors and aroma better than just leaving coffee to cool at room temperature or in the fridge. For a beautiful effect, especially when entertaining, serve in a tall martini glass without ice cubes.

* Brands may vary by region; substitute a similar product.

Café Rumba
EQUAL ▲

1 cup heavy whipping cream
1 teaspoon pure vanilla extract
6 packets Equal sweetener
1 teaspoon rum extract
4 cups freshly brewed dark-roast coffee
Ground cinnamon (optional)

1. Beat whipping cream until fluffy. Add vanilla and 3 packets of Equal and continue to beat until soft peaks form.

2. Divide the whipped cream among 4 cups.

3. Stir remaining 3 packets of Equal and rum extract into the brewed coffee. Pour coffee over the whipped cream.

4. Garnish with a sprinkle of cinnamon. Makes 4 servings.

Tip: This is also delicious with 1 ounce of aged rum per cup in place of the rum extract.

Recipe developed by Tony Abou-Ganim, mixologist on the Fine Living Network.

Café Bueno
KIRKLAND SIGNATURE

8 cups water
1/3 cup firmly packed brown sugar
2 whole cloves
1 cinnamon stick
8 ounces whipping cream
1 ounce unsweetened baking chocolate
1 cup Kirkland Signature ground coffee
1 teaspoon vanilla extract

1. Pour water into a medium saucepan and bring to a boil over medium heat. Stir in brown sugar, cloves and cinnamon stick, broken in half. Reduce the heat and simmer for 15 minutes.

2. While the mixture simmers, whip cream until it forms soft peaks. Hold in the refrigerator.

3. Remove brown sugar/spice mixture from the heat. Add chocolate and stir until melted.

4. Add ground coffee, cover and let stand for 5 minutes. Stir in vanilla.

5. Strain mixture through cheesecloth or a coffee filter.

6. Serve immediately in coffee mugs, garnished with whipping cream. Makes 8 servings.

Cranberry Punch
KIRKLAND SIGNATURE/CLIFFSTAR

4 cups Kirkland Signature Cranberry Cocktail, chilled
1 cup orange juice, chilled
1/4 teaspoon orange extract
12 ounces lemon-lime soda, chilled
1 pint raspberry sherbet, slightly softened

1. Mix cranberry cocktail, orange juice and orange extract.

2. Just before serving, add the soda.

3. Pour mixture into individual serving glasses and top with a tablespoon of sherbet. Makes 12 servings.

Brunch Punch
UNIFRUTTI/ANTHONY VINEYARDS/
CAL SALES-KIRSCHENMAN

2 midnight oranges*
2 cups green seedless grapes*, quartered
6 kiwis*, peeled and quartered
12 navel oranges*, juiced
1 1-liter bottle lemon-lime soda
Sliced kiwi, for garnish (optional)

1. Slice midnight oranges, place in a ring mold and fill mold with water. Freeze overnight.
2. Puree grapes and kiwis in a blender. Strain through a sieve if desired.
3. Pour grape/kiwi mixture, orange juice and soda into a punch bowl.
4. Garnish with midnight orange ring and kiwi slices. Makes 12 servings.

Recipe created by Linda Carey, culinary specialist.
* Brands may vary by region; substitute a similar product.

Appleberry Blast
TREE TOP

1 ¹/₂ cups Tree Top* Apple Juice
1 cup frozen strawberries or frozen mixed berries (raspberries, strawberries and blueberries)
¹/₂ cup vanilla ice cream or frozen yogurt, or vanilla yogurt
¹/₄ teaspoon ground cinnamon (optional)

1. Combine all ingredients in a blender.
2. Cover and blend at high speed until smooth. Makes 2 servings.

* Brands may vary by region; substitute a similar product.

Pomegranate Cooler
LANGERS JUICE ▲

¹/₄ cup Langers All Pomegranate Juice
¹/₄ cup lemon-lime soda
¹/₄ cup freshly squeezed lime juice
Lime wedge, for garnish

1. Combine pomegranate juice, soda and lime juice.
2. Serve over ice and garnish with a lime wedge. Makes 1 serving.

Recipe created by Linda Carey, culinary specialist.

Mango Shake
PROFOOD ▲

1 cup vanilla ice cream
2 cups milk/soy milk
2 cups Philippine Brand* dried mangoes
1 cup ice

1. Combine ice cream and milk in a bowl.
2. Add mangoes and let soak for 30-45 minutes in the refrigerator.
3. Pour mixture into a blender, add ice and blend until it reaches the consistency of a shake. Makes 4 servings.

* Brands may vary by region; substitute a similar product.

ENJOY THE PERFECT CUP OF COFFEE AT HOME

You're off to a good start by selecting high-quality, perfectly roasted beans from Starbucks. But there's more to great coffee than picking the right beans. You'll also need to store, grind and brew those beans properly. The good news: this is all very easy.

1. Match the correct grind to your coffeemaker.

The coffee-brewing method you use at home – press, drip or espresso – dictates how finely your coffee should be ground. Coffee presses require a coarse grind. Espresso machines require a very fine grind. Drip coffeemakers fall in between those two.

2. Proportion is important.

Too much water, and you have a weak brew. Too little, and you may find it undrinkable. We recommend 2 Tbsp (10g) ground coffee for every 6 fl oz (180mL) of water. If you decide that's too strong, you can always add hot water after brewing.

3. Use fresh, cold water.

With so much attention paid to selecting and grinding the beans, it's easy to forget the importance of good water. The water you have at home should be clean, fresh and free of impurities. If your local tap water isn't up to snuff, then consider filtered or bottled water.

4. Proper storage will help maintain the freshness and flavor of your coffee.

Coffee is an agricultural product which means it will be at the peak of freshness for only about a week after the FlavorLock™ bag is opened. You can keep your coffee fresher (and tasting better) longer by storing whole beans in a dry, dark place. An airtight, opaque container kept at room temperature is best.

5. Serve coffee at the peak of flavor and freshness.

Boiling produces bitter coffee; it should be brewed between 195°F and 205°F (90°C and 96°C) to extract the full range of flavors. After brewing, you can keep it on a burner for only 20 minutes or so before it becomes unpleasant. A thermal carafe will keep coffee hot and delicious for much longer periods of time. And never reheat coffee – that just makes it taste bad.

WITH THE RIGHT COFFEE AND THE PROPER TECHNIQUES, YOU'RE ON YOUR WAY TO BREWING THE PERFECT CUP.

Index I

Index I

Index

Vendor listing I

C&R FARMS, 46

CAL SALES/KIRSCHENMAN, 65, 211
559-741-7030

CALAVO GROWERS, 29, 45
www.calavo.com
800-4-CALAVO (22-5286)

CALIFORNIA AVOCADO
COMMISSION, 29, 45
www.avocado.org

CAMANCHACA, 125
www.camanchacainc.com
800-335-7553

CAMPBELL'S, 158
www.campbellselect.com
800-257-8443

CARDILE BROTHERS, 170
cardilebro@aol.com
610-268-2470

CARGILL, 101, 102, 103
www.cargillmeatsolutions.com
877-596-4069

CASTLE ROCK VINEYARDS, 56
msabovich@castlerockvine yards.com
661-721-8717

CHELAN FRESH, 120
www.chelanfresh.com
509-682-3854

CHERRY CENTRAL, 167
www.cherrycentral.com

CHESTNUT HILL FARMS, 121
www.chfusa.com

CHICKEN OF THE SEA, 158
www.chickenofthesea.com

CHILEAN AVOCADO IMPORTERS
ASSOC., 29, 45
202-626-0560

CIBO NATURALS, 159
www.cibonaturals.com
800-823-2426

CLEAR SPRINGS, 137
www.clearsprings.com
csf@clearsprings.com
800-635-8211

COLUMBIA MARKETING
INTERNATIONAL, 162, 163
www.cmiapples.com
509-663-1955

CONAGRA, 125, 180
www.conagrafoods.com
813-241-1500

COTTAGE BAKERY, 160, 203
info@cottagebakery.com
209-333-8044

COUNTRYSIDE BAKING, 189
800-478-4252

CREATE A TREAT, 188
myhouse@createatreat.com

CURRY & COMPANY, 204
www.curryandco.com

D'ARRIGO BROS. OF CA., 51
www.andyboy.com
800-995-5939

DANNON, 200
www.dannon.com
877-326-6668

DEL MONTE, 124
www.delmonte.com

DEL MONTE FRESH, 23
Jbohmer@freshdelmonte.com
305-520-8118

DEL REY AVOCADO, 29, 45
760-728-8325

DELANO FARMS, 20, 21, 22
delfarm@delanofarmsco.com
661-721-1485

DELTA PRIDE, 138, 139
www.deltapride.com

DENICE & FILICE, LLC, 48
www.denicefilice.com
831-630-6000

DIAMOND FOODS, INC., 42
www.diamondfoods.com
www.emeraldnuts.com

DIAMOND FRUIT GROWERS, 44
www.diamondfruit.com
541-354-5300

DIMARE FRESH, 31
www.dimarefresh.com

DIVINE FLAVOR, 140
www.divineflavor.com
619-710-2020

DNE WORLD FRUIT, 166
www.dneworld.com
800-327-6676

DOLE, 110, 111
www.dole.com
800-232-8888

DOLE MUSHROOMS, 146
www.dolemushroom.com
info@dolemushrooms.com
866-355-2077

DOMEX, 150
www.superapple.com
domex@superapple.com
509-966-1814

Vendor listing I

Vendor listing

Vendor listing

WALLACE FARMS, 68
sales@wallacespuds.com
360-757-0981

WELCH'S, 131
www.welchs.com

WESPAK, 44
www.wespak.com
sales@wpemail.com
559-897-4800

WEST PAK, 29, 45
www.westpakavocado.com
matt@westpakavocado.com
951-296-5757

WESTERN SWEET CHERRY,
121, 189
509-972-4476

**WESTERN UNITED FISH
COMPANY,** 140
www.wufco.net
westernunited@wufco.net
206-763-1227

WILCOX FARMS, 10, 11
www.wilcoxfarms.com

WILSONBATIZ, 149
www.wilsonbatiz.com
619-710-2020

WINDSET FARMS, 63
www.windsetfarms.com

**WOLVERINE PACKING
COMPANY,** 118
www.wolverinepacking.com
800-521-1390

YAKIMA-ROCHE FRUIT, 19
509-453-4000

Notes

Notes